# God Built

# God Built

Forged by God ... in the Bad and Good of Life

## Steve Farrar

David C Cook®

*transforming lives together*

GOD BUILT
Published by David C. Cook
4050 Lee Vance View
Colorado Springs, CO 80918 U.S.A.

David C. Cook Distribution Canada
55 Woodslee Avenue, Paris, Ontario, Canada N3L 3E5

David C. Cook U.K., Kingsway Communications
Eastbourne, East Sussex BN23 6NT, England

David C. Cook and the graphic circle C logo
are registered trademarks of Cook Communications Ministries.

Unless otherwise noted, Scripture quotations are taken from the *New American Standard Bible*, © Copyright 1960, 1995 by The Lockman Foundation. Used by permission. Scripture quotations marked NIV taken from the *Holy Bible, New International Version*®. *NIV*®. Copyright © 1973, 1978, 1984 International Bible Society. Used by permission of Zondervan. All rights reserved; ESV are taken from *The Holy Bible, English Standard Version*. Copyright © 2000; 2001 by Crossway Bibles, a division of Good News Publishers. Used by permission. All rights reserved; AB are taken from *The Amplified Bible*. Copyright © 1954, 1958, 1962, 1964, 1965, 1987 by The Lockman Foundation. Used by permission; and NKJV are taken from the New King James Version. Copyright © 1982 by Thomas Nelson, Inc. Used by permission. All rights reserved. Italics in Scripture quotations have been added by the author for emphasis.

LCCN 2008927719
Hardcover ISBN 978-1-4347-6850-6
International Trade Paperback Edition ISBN 978-1-4347-6727-1

© 2008 Steve Farrar
Published in association with the literary agency of
WordServe Literary Group, Ltd., 10152 S. Knoll Circle, Highlands Ranch, CO 80130

The Team: Don Pape, Larry Libby, Amy Kiechlin, Jack Campbell, and Susan Vannaman
Cover Design: The DesignWorks Group, David Uttley

Printed in the United States of America
First Edition 2008

1 2 3 4 5 6 7 8 9 10

050608

# Contents

# The Story of Joseph from 30,000 Feet

## (A Guaranteed 15-Minute Read)

*If you happen to be well familiar with the account of Joseph in the book of Genesis, this will be a quick flyover at 30,000 feet. On the other hand, if you're new to the Bible and don't know much about this guy, this will be an introductory flyover at 30,000 feet. But if you want to set aside some time, open your Bible to Genesis 37 and read through chapter 50, you'll get the full-meal deal, and you'll be congratulating yourself for years to come. Okay ... we're airborne. Settle into your window seat and check out some unforgettable landscape....*

Joseph had eleven brothers, and at least ten of them hated his guts.

He came from a messed-up family with a now-famous pedigree. Some people trace their lineage back to the *Mayflower*; Joseph traced his lineage back to the great patriarch and father of all the Jews, Abraham. Abraham was his great-grandfather, Isaac was his grandfather, and Jacob was his father. Throughout the Bible you will read the phrase "The God of Abraham, Isaac, and Jacob." That's a big deal, and Joseph was part of that privileged line.

So why did the ten brothers hate this young man so deeply? That requires a little bit of background that goes back to Joseph's father, Jacob. Jacob fathered twelve boys. In addition to the twelve sons, Jacob had one daughter, Dinah.

These thirteen kids had the same father but four different mothers. And that's where most of the trouble began.

Jacob had been tricked into marrying Leah when he really wanted to marry Rachel, but on his wedding night he must have knocked down a few too many shots of Jacobus Daniel's malt whiskey. He thought he was marrying Rachel, but he woke up with Leah. Laban, the father of Leah and Rachel, had conned Jacob big-time. Jacob could normally out-slick just about anyone, but he met his match with Laban.

Since Rachel was the love of his life, Jacob decided to renegotiate his contract with Laban. He had worked seven years to get beautiful Rachel, and now he was married to the not-so-beautiful Leah. Laban offered him a deal, giving him permission to marry Rachel the following week—but he had to work for seven more years. Since Jacob was no longer a free agent, he didn't have much choice except to agree to Laban's terms.

So Jacob signed off and now he had two wives. When the two girls were married to Jacob, their father gave each of them a servant. Rachel was given a young woman named Bilhah, and Leah was given Zilpah.

There's a reason that I bring this up.

Jacob's thirteen kids would come from these four women.

And that's why Joseph's ten brothers hated him so much.

## Family Feud

Joseph was the firstborn by Rachel, and then later Rachel died giving birth to his little brother, Benjamin. Joseph and Benjamin got along just fine, but the other brothers couldn't stand the sight of Joseph. After all, Rachel was the love of Jacob's life, and Joseph was the firstborn by Rachel. For years and years, Rachel was unable to have children. And then, unexpectedly, when Jacob was an older man, she became pregnant with Joseph. Joseph was the son of his old age (and Benjamin would be the son of his older age). For all these reasons, Joseph was the hands-down favorite of Dad. And all the brothers knew it.

When Jacob gave Joseph the new field coat from LL Bean and didn't get one for the other boys—well, that certainly didn't help things. All that did was fuel the raging fire of jealousy.

And then, on two separate occasions, young Joseph had prophetic dreams. In the first dream, bundles (sheaves) of wheat in the harvest field were bowing down before Joseph's sheaf. When he told the dream to his brothers, it really hacked them off. The message was pretty clear, and these brothers didn't miss it. Mocking the young man for his dreams, they let Joseph know that Hades would freeze over before they bowed before *him*.

Sometime later he had a second dream, and this time the sun, the moon, and eleven stars were bowing down before him. When he told this second dream to his brothers, they went ballistic. Even Jacob was taken aback by the message and the thought that they might all bow before Joseph one day. But Jacob didn't dismiss the dream—he just put it on the back burner and let it simmer.

This is why the ten brothers were so insanely jealous of Joseph.

And it also explains why they tried to kill him when he was seventeen years old.

## Let's Make a Deal

The brothers were pasturing the sheep up north in Shechem where there was more rainfall and more grassland. Jacob wanted to know how the ten brothers were getting along and how the sheep were doing, so he told Joseph to go north and check things out and then bring him back a report.

Joseph was going to take a road trip. Road trips are a big deal when you're seventeen, and this was going to be a long one—somewhere in the range of seventy to eighty miles. That was a huge event in Israel three thousand years ago. Normally Joseph didn't get more than three or four miles away from home, and he always had to be home by eleven.

Joseph headed north, and when he got to Shechem, a man told him that his brothers had headed west to Dothan. That didn't bother Joseph a bit. It meant he got to extend his trip by another twenty or thirty miles, and play around with his new GPS receiver.

Apparently Joseph's brothers saw him before he saw them, because they spotted him when he was still quite a distance away. And they immediately knew that this was their opportunity to take him out. The brothers quickly got in a huddle and decided that they would kill him and then throw him into a pit. Who would know? Who would find out? They would simply send word to their dad that a wild animal had killed Joseph.

Reuben was the oldest brother, and felt at least a measure of responsibility in the family. He talked the other guys out of killing the kid. So they threw Joseph into a pit while they took a dinner break. They chewed on their hummus burgers, chased it with goat's milk, and kicked around the best way they could do away with Joseph.

It was Reuben's plan to sneak back around, pull Joseph out of the pit, and send him home. But while Reuben was absent, the other brothers saw a Midianite slave caravan going by, and that's when Judah got what he and the other guys thought was a brilliant idea. Judah convinced the brothers not to kill Joseph but to sell him to the slavers and make some quick cash to pay the Visa bill. They would then cover up their crime by taking his coat of many colors, dipping it in goat's blood, and telling Dad that the Lion King had ambushed Joseph.

It was the perfect crime!

So that's precisely what they did. They sold Joseph into a life of slavery for twenty shekels of silver.

When Reuben came back to rescue Little Joe and send him back to the Ponderosa, he was long gone. He was history, and now they would never have to deal with this irritating kid again. He was finally out of their lives.

Forever.

Or so they thought.

## Meanwhile … in Egypt

When Jacob saw Joseph's coat soaked in blood, he mourned for his boy with a broken heart. He knew he would never completely recover from Joseph's death. That would be a burden he knew he would carry for the rest of his life. One day he would die with a heart that had never healed.

While Jacob grieved for the son he thought was dead, Joseph went up for sale in Egypt to a high-ranking government official by the name of Potiphar. As far as Joseph knew, he was going to be a slave for the rest of his life. Slaves have a lot of job security—but not much of a future.

At seventeen, Joseph's life was over.

Joseph now belonged to a guy with the weird name of Potiphar, a prominent government official in the big time of Egyptian politics. He basically ran the Secret Service for Pharaoh. He was a major player in Pharaoh's cabinet, with all the expected perks of power, connections, and wealth.

Potiphar was a successful man with a new slave who was about to become an unbelievable success. But nobody knew that when Joseph first showed up in chains. The Bible says that "the Lord was with Joseph and he became a successful man." Slaves don't become successful men. Slaves get used up and die young.

But something remarkable began to happen as Joseph went about his duties as a slave. Whatever he touched seemed to turn to gold. Joseph pulled off every task he was given with an air of elegance and class, always going the extra mile for his master. As he was faithful in little, he soon became faithful in much. His superiors kept promoting him, and his achievements were so notable that Potiphar began to watch him closely.

What was with this kid? Everything attached to Joseph's work was a home run. He was given more and more responsibility, and it got to the point that even Potiphar, an Egyptian pagan, could tell that the Lord was with Joseph.

Then the unthinkable happened. Potiphar promoted Joseph and put him in charge of his entire house.

And this was no ordinary house.

Potiphar ruled over a large, prosperous estate that demanded a lot of oversight. And in a move that must have stunned Joseph himself, Potiphar handed over the entire operation—land, slaves, the works—to this young Hebrew slave. Before long, Joseph was signing checks and running QuickBooks. Potiphar trusted Joseph with everything he owned—and it all kept growing and turning a profit under his leadership.

Joseph had to be astonished and grateful for God's goodness. He came to Egypt as a slave, and now he was overseeing all the operations of a great and impressive estate. With that remarkable promotion came an increase in power, privilege, and possessions for Joseph. It was the original rags to riches story.

But there was one snag.

Potiphar had a wife who wanted to sleep with Joseph.

## Desperate Housewife

The Bible says that Joseph was handsome in form and appearance—in other words, he was fit and buff. He had recently completed the Nile Triathlon. Joseph was probably in his late twenties when this rich, evidently bored Egyptian chick decided she wanted an affair with her husband's main man.

She propositioned Joseph (well, actually *commanded* Joseph), and the young man's classic response revealed the character of his heart: "How could I do this great evil and sin against God?"

He also made it very clear to the trophy wife that her husband had put him in charge of the entire estate and had withheld nothing from him—except her. There was no way he was going to violate Potiphar's trust. So he refused her offer—but she refused to take no for an answer. Day after day she offered herself to Joseph, and day after day he refused to give in, doing his best to avoid her.

Finally, in frustration, she set a trap for him, and actually got her hands on him. But Joseph tore away from her grasp and literally ran away—leaving his coat behind. The deceitful woman then used the coat as evidence when she accused Joseph of trying to rape her—and the next thing Joseph knew he was in jail.

Was Joseph in jail for doing what was wrong? No. He had done what was right. It was a real blow to Joseph to lose his great position with Potiphar. And now he was doing time (and who knew how much time) for a crime he didn't commit.

But the Lord was still with him. And that's why Joseph found favor with the chief jailer.

## Get Out of Jail Free

Within a very short time, the chief jailer had handed the entire operation of the prison over to Joseph. Did you get that? Joseph had been sent to jail—and now he was running the place! And he ran that prison system with integrity and class, just as he had managed the great estate. Once again, his life had been rescued and resurrected.

A short time after Joseph's promotion, two important servants of Pharaoh were thrown into prison. On the same night, they both had dreams, and Joseph interpreted the dreams. He told the chief cupbearer that in three days he would be reinstated to his favored post. The news to the chief baker was that in three days he would be hanged. And that's precisely what happened.

As the chief cupbearer was summoned back to Pharaoh three days later, Joseph said to him, "Don't forget me. Mention me to Pharaoh, and get me out of here."

The man *immediately* forgot Joseph, who remained in double captivity—slavery and jail—for two more years.

Then one night as those two years were drawing to a close, it was Pharaoh's turn to have a disturbing dream. It was one of those wild, crazy dreams that didn't make sense—but somehow Pharaoh knew it was more than that.

The first part of the dream was about seven fat cows and seven lean, emaciated cows. Then he woke up, shook it off, and went back to sleep. He thought the dream was over, but it was only halftime. When he went back to sleep this time, he dreamt about seven full stalks of grain, followed by seven withered stalks.

Waking up the next morning, before anyone had their first cup of coffee, he pulled all of his advisers together to figure out the meaning of the dreams. But nobody had a clue. That's when the cupbearer suddenly remembered Joseph. He told Pharaoh about the time Joseph interpreted his dream—and how the interpretation was spot-on. Immediately, Pharaoh gave the word to bring this Joseph before the throne.

Joseph jumped in the shower, shaved, and within the hour found himself standing before the most powerful king on the earth. Not only did he tell Pharaoh that the dreams meant God would be sending seven years of prosperity to be followed by seven years of extreme famine, but he also gave the king a battle plan. The essential message? Save 20 percent of the grain during the fat years, and you'll get through the famine.

Joseph recommended that Pharaoh find a manager, a man he could put in charge of the whole operation, and Pharaoh said, "I think I've already found him. You're the man!"

## Guess Who's Coming to Dinner

In the space of about forty-five minutes, Joseph went from the lowest place in Egypt to the highest. Just that fast, he was made co-ruler with Pharaoh and became the second most powerful man on the face of the earth.

Seven years went by—seven good, rich years—and then the famine hit, just as Joseph had predicted. And before long, guess who showed up in Egypt to buy grain?

You guessed it. The ten bad brothers.

Jacob had sent them south to get provisions—but kept young Benjamin home with him, fearful that some type of harm might come to him on the trip.

When the brothers showed up in Egypt to get the grain, they had no idea they were dealing with Joseph. How could they have known? This guy looked like a pharaoh and spoke to them through an interpreter. Joseph recognized them right off the bat, and when they all bowed down before him, the Bible says, "Joseph remembered the dreams which he had about them."

As he interrogated them, Joseph found out that his dad was still alive back in Canaan, and that his younger brother, Benjamin, was still at home. Joseph fooled his brothers by accusing them of being spies, and locked them up in prison for three days. When he finally let them go, he told them they could prove they weren't spies by going home and coming back with Benjamin, their little brother. In the meantime, he would hold Simeon in prison.

Just to give them a little indigestion on the trip home, Joseph secretly had the money that they had paid for the grain put back in the grain sacks they were taking home.

On the way back, they stopped at a Starbucks and one of the brothers opened a grain bag to give some to his donkey. That's when he found the money. The other brothers checked their bags and they all found their cash. At this point, they were all on the verge of a nervous breakdown.

The brothers were horrified—and they knew in their hearts that God was now dealing out punishment to them for what they had done to Joseph years before. Although the Bible hadn't been written yet, they were encountering the truth Moses wrote centuries on down the road: "You may be sure that your sin will find you out" (Num. 32:23 NIV).

The brothers returned home—minus Simeon—to report to their father what had happened. They had to go back to Egypt with Benjamin—but they couldn't go back, because Jacob flatly refused. But then as the famine ground on and on, he finally had no choice. He sent the guys—with Benjamin in tow—back to Egypt. They were also going back to return double the cash that was in their sacks (Jacob's idea).

When Joseph saw they had returned with Benjamin, he invited them to a great banquet, seating them in the exact order of their birth. The brothers were stunned. What were the odds of something like that happening? And Joseph gave Benjamin five times the amount of food that the others had at their plates.

When Joseph came into the banquet and the brothers bowed before him again, and when Joseph met with Benjamin … it got to be too much. Joseph had to quickly leave the room to control his emotions. After composing himself, he returned to the banquet, and they ate their meal together. They talked a little football, a little politics, and then everyone turned in.

The brothers imagined that everything was cool now, and that the whole crazy affair with the assistant pharaoh was over.

How wrong they were.

## "I Am Joseph!"

The next morning Joseph's steward loaded their donkeys with grain and cash, but at Joseph's command, he also put Joseph's silver cup in Benjamin's sack. As the men left Egypt, they were relieved to have the ordeal behind them. But they weren't too far from the city when Joseph sent his security unit after them.

Needless to say, they were stunned at the accusation of stealing this Egyptian's silver cup. Even so, when a search was made and it was found in Benjamin's sack, the other brothers knew the jig was up. God was repaying them for their terrible act of selling Joseph into slavery.

When they returned to the city, they again bowed low before Joseph. Judah appealed to him, pleading for mercy. He explained that if Benjamin didn't return, it would kill their father, since he had already grieved for years over the death of another son.

Joseph ordered everyone out of the room except his brothers. And then he declared to them, "I am Joseph!"

The brothers had to be in a state of paralyzed shock.

Then Joseph quickly told them they shouldn't be angry with themselves— which was a statement of magnificent mercy. He then told them that God had sent him to Egypt in order to preserve life—theirs included.

He invited them to return home, gather up their dad and their families, and join him in Egypt. There were still five years left in the famine, and he would make provision for all of them—and he would build homes for them in a gated subdivision called Goshen.

So they returned home, told the news to their astonished father, picked up the wives and kids, and moved to Egypt to join Joseph.

It was a great day when Jacob was reunited with his long-lost son, Joseph. They would have seventeen years together, renewing the relationship of the years that had been stolen from them. And then the day came when Jacob, the father of twelve boys who would become the twelve tribes of Israel, died.

When Jacob died, the ten brothers panicked.

Why did they panic?

They were convinced that now Joseph would turn on them and take revenge for what they had done to him years earlier. Joseph was now forty-nine and virtually the most powerful man on the face of the earth. He could do whatever he wanted to get even with them for what they did to him when he was seventeen.

In their panic, they sent a message to Joseph that basically said, "Hey, Joseph, we forgot to tell you that before Dad died he wanted to make sure that you would forgive us for what we did to you."

When Joseph heard this, he wept.

He knew the hearts of his brothers and what was behind the message.

They were scared to death that he was going to draw and quarter them like Braveheart (even though that was twenty-five hundred years later).

Joseph's response to them showed his perspective on all that had happened to him. He said to them, "Do not be afraid, for am I in God's place?"

In other words, you guys don't need to be afraid, because God was overseeing all that happened. How did I get to be the most powerful man on the face of the earth? Was it my network or my education? No, it was God Himself who put me here. As for you, you intended it for evil, but God meant it for good to bring about this present result, to preserve many people alive.

So don't worry, I'm not against you, I'm for you. I will continue to take care of you and your families. And with those words, Joseph was kind and merciful to the brothers who had plotted his death and sold him into a life of slavery.

Joseph uttered those words at the age of 49. He would live a long life and die at the age of 110. Over four hundred years later, when Moses led the people out of Egypt, they carried with them the bones of Joseph and buried them in the Promised Land, the land of Abraham, Isaac, and Jacob.

And that's the story of Joseph from 30,000 feet.

Now, back on the ground again, we get to dive into a strong river of truth that runs from here to eternity … with a few class-5 rapids along the way.

It should be quite a ride.

Chapter One

# Strangely and Slowly, God Is Working

*"Sovereign Ruler of the skies,*
*Ever gracious, ever wise,*
*All my times are in thy hand,*
*All events at thy command."*
*—John Rylands*

I f anyone has even been a victim, it was Joseph.

America seems full of "victims" today. Have you noticed? Everyone is a victim and everyone is looking for payback.

Joseph was a *legitimate* victim. If he were alive today, his tragic story would land him on *Oprah*. And she wouldn't have him on just for a day; she would tell his story over the course of an entire week. The tears would be flowing and the Kleenex would be three feet deep in the studio audience. Psychologists would be brought in to explain Joseph's trauma.

But at the age of forty-nine as he faced his brothers, Joseph wasn't in trauma. He wasn't bitter, and he didn't have road rage.

To put it mildly, this was *not* what they had anticipated. They were expecting Joseph to do to them what they would have done to him had the tables been turned. But instead of torturing, jailing, or killing them outright—Joseph was *kind* to them.

These guys just didn't get it. They had nothing but fear in their hearts toward Joseph, because they really didn't know Joseph—or Joseph's God. Because they didn't fear God, they were afraid of their brother.

Joseph had learned to fear the Lord, and as a result, he spoke a soothing and forgiving word to those fearful brothers. Joseph was a man of God instead of a man of the world. He had no thought here of revenge or payback.

In every family, someone needs to grow up.

In every family, someone needs to get over it.

In every family, someone needs to become mature and forgive.

They deserved payback, all right. They deserved everything they were so afraid of. But they didn't get it. And that must have shocked them beyond words.

Why didn't they receive their "just deserts"? Because they had a brother who was a mature man, neither bitter nor vindictive. He wasn't looking to intimidate, sue, or extract his pound of flesh.

He was compassionate and kind to those who sought to destroy him. He provided for them financially and for their children.

There is nothing in Joseph's life that points to his being a victim.

That's because he wasn't a victim.

He was a victor.

## From Victim to Victor

So how did he make the transition from victim to victor? Only one doctrine enables us to travel that road, and it's a truth Joseph embraced with his whole heart.

That doctrine is the sovereignty and providence of God.

What that means in plain language is this: God is a BIG GOD. Probably much bigger than you think.

These are two rich gold mines of truth that have been sadly ignored and lost in the lives of most Christians. If someone offered you a producing gold mine for free, you would immediately start looking for the "catch." But let's just say there is no catch, and as a matter of fact, that same someone is offering you not one free gold mine but two.

That's what we're talking about here.

The two gold mines given to us are twin truths: We have a have a BIG GOD who works *sovereignly* and *providentially* in our lives. And catch this—in order to make the internal U-turn in your heart from a victim to a victor, you have to anchor your life on these two truths. They are absolutely essential for your survival. Without the sovereignty and providence of God, you will always remain a victim. But when you discover the truth of these attributes of your heavenly Father, it throws the events of your life into a completely different light.

The sovereignty and providence of God are like two sides of a coin, inescapably linked together. Sovereignty and providence go hand in hand. And it's a great tragedy that these powerful twin truths have been lost to this generation.

So what do they mean?

Joseph said to his brothers, "Am I in God's place?" In the midst of their fear he says, "Wait a minute, guys. How do you think I got into this position of power and authority? Do you think it was random chance?" He didn't get it through luck, he didn't get it through his résumé, and he didn't get it because he was well connected. He was there because God, from before the foundation of the world, had planned for Joseph to be there. He was there because it was God's place for him, and God had sovereignly and providentially placed him in that great palace.

It wasn't coincidence.

It wasn't chance.

It wasn't the luck of the draw.

God had determined that he be in that position from before the worlds were created. That's how he got there. Joseph took no credit for his position. He knew it came from the hand of the Lord.

So what is the sovereignty of God?

Sovereignty contains three key ideas: ownership, authority, and control.[1] God created it all, He owns it all, He is over all, and He controls it all. That was true of human kings who owned and controlled their turf, as well, but Jesus, remember, is the *King* of Kings. And that means He owns every king, He is over every king, and He controls every king in history—past, present, and future, because He has created every king. In other words, HE IS IN CONTROL.

Let me throw a few verses at you that teach this truth with a lot of concrete:

> For I know that the LORD is great
> And that our Lord is above all gods.
> Whatever the LORD pleases, He does,
> In heaven and in earth, in the seas and in all deeps.
> (Ps. 135:5–6)

> But our God is in the heavens;
> He does whatever He pleases.
> (Ps. 115:3)

> The LORD has established His throne in the heavens,
> And His sovereignty rules over all.
> (Ps. 103:19)

> The earth is the LORD's, and all it contains,
> The world, and those who dwell in it.
> For He has founded it upon the seas
> And established it upon the rivers.
> (Ps. 24:1–2)

This is a BIG GOD. Big beyond the universe He created. Bigger than we could ever understand. This God is in complete control. He not only controls the movements of galaxies and multiple trillions of stars, He is also in control of you, your life, and everything that happens in your life.

Does that rub you the wrong way? For most of us, it does. The absolute sovereignty of God is a feisty capsule that tends to stick in our throats and cause us great discomfort. But this is a truth that you've got to wash down, so you can digest it and live your life off it.

The great Bible scholar B. B. Warfield describes the root of our discomfort. I have to tell you that I really like this man. He doesn't mess around, and he isn't boring like a lot of guys who teach theology. He shoots straight—and he throws fastballs high and inside.

> We wish "to belong to ourselves," and we resent belonging, especially belonging absolutely, to anybody else, even if that anybody else be God. We are in the mood of the singer of the hymn beginning, "I was a wandering sheep," when he declares himself, "I would not be controlled." We will not be controlled. Or rather, to speak more accurately, we will not admit that we are controlled.
>
> I say that it is more accurate to say that we will not admit that we are controlled. For we are controlled, whether we admit it or not. To imagine that we are not controlled is to imagine that there is no God. For when we say God, we say control. If a single creature which God has made has escaped beyond his control, at the moment that he has done so he has abolished God. A God who could or would make such a creature whom he could not or would not control, is no God. The moment he should make such a creature he would, of course, abdicate his throne. The universe he had created would have ceased to be his universe; or rather it

would cease to exist, for the universe is held together only by the control of God.[2]

The sovereignty of God means that He is in control—*of everything.* That's why He is a BIG GOD. And that's why He is a GREAT GOD.

This means that when we look around and get the very strong sense that the world and our lives are out of control, we are wrong. It may appear to us that events have jumped the tracks and headed over the cliff, but in truth they are moving absolutely on schedule according to His divine plan and purpose.

It was John Flavel who said to his congregation in England, some three hundred years ago, "Some providences of God, like Hebrew letters, are best understood backwards."

English reads left to right. Hebrew reads right to left. So to us, Hebrew reads backward.

So, too, does the providence of God.

Some chapters of our lives make absolutely no sense. We get blindsided by some tragedy, and we wonder where God is. It just doesn't add up! Where is this God who loves me, and why has He allowed this to happen? You and I can ask those kinds of questions over and over again, but the fact of the matter is that these confusing chapters won't make sense while we're in the middle of them.

In these bewildering chapters of life you will have to give five, ten, or even twenty years before things begin to make sense. Only then, like Joseph looking backward, do some providences of God become crystal clear. When we look backward, we see that God was in control even when it looked like our lives were out of control. Oftentimes, we can't see that providence until we get through the storm and look behind us. You look back and can't believe you survived the ferocity of that storm. But you did. And it was all due to the goodness and plan of God.

That plan in the midst of the storm could not be seen. In fact, at times, it seemed like God had abandoned you. Job knew what that was like. In his great loss and despair, he couldn't find God anywhere:

Oh that I knew where I might find Him,
That I might come to His seat!
I would present my case before Him
And fill my mouth with arguments....
Behold, I go forward but He is not there,
And backward, but I cannot perceive Him;
When He acts on the left, I cannot behold Him;
He turns on the right, I cannot see Him.
(Job 23:3–4, 8–9)

That must have been what Joseph experienced as he took that long camel ride—his chains clanking every step of the way—down to Egypt and a life of never-ending slavery.

The sovereignty of God means that He is King and He is in absolute control; and it also means that we are not.

Joseph addressed his brothers not as a victim but as a victor. How could he not be caught up in bitterness and revenge? When he looked back over his life, he saw the absolute control of God working His eternal plan in every event of his life—the good and the bad. It was all under the sovereign control of the great God of Israel.

So what about providence?

Providence is God's execution of His plan in your life and in the entire universe. Have you ever heard the saying "the devil is in the details"? That is absolutely incorrect.

God is in the details.

O Lord, you are my God;
I will exalt you; I will praise your name,
for you have done wonderful things,
plans formed of old, faithful and sure.
(Isa. 25:1 esv)

Are these plans that God hurriedly drew up last night to fix something in your life that has gone wrong? Is God looking for some "Plan B" because "Plan A" didn't pan out for us? No. These are plans that He purposed before He created the world. God hasn't been up all night—papers and maps spread out across the floor of heaven, amending His purposes to fit our present set of circumstances. No, the plans He has for you are His original plans. Perfect plans that never need to be amended. Now that's a BIG GOD.

The plans He has made are always executed perfectly. His plan is sure. It is not uncertain. In order for His plan to be executed and accomplished, He micromanages your life and the entire universe. He carries it all, sustains it all, and keeps it all going. And that can only be done if One is in absolute control. But He is in control, and that's why Job 23:14 states, "He performs what is appointed for me."

God's plan for your life is going to happen—on time and on schedule. John J. Murray sums it up well:

> The plan of God is perfect.
> The plan is exhaustive.
> The plan is for my ultimate good.
> The plan is secret. God hides it from me until it happens.
> I discover it day by day as it unfolds.[3]

In essence, the doctrine of providence teaches that which God creates, He continually provides for and sustains—and that means *you*. He created you, and He will continually provide for you and sustain you—that's how He pulls off His plan in your life. Hebrews 1:3 declares that Christ "upholds all things by the word of His power." The English Standard Version, another excellent translation, states that Christ "upholds the universe by the word of his power."

What does this BIG GOD of ours do all day? Dr. Wayne Grudem gives us a glimpse of how God invests His time:

The Greek word translated "upholding" is *phero*, "carry, bear." This is commonly used in the New Testament for carrying something from one place to another, such as bringing a paralyzed man to Jesus (Luke 5:18), or bringing a cloak and books to Paul (2 Timothy 4:13). It does not simply mean "sustain." … In Hebrews 1:3, [the grammar] indicates that Jesus is continually carrying along all things, "in the universe by the word of His power."

Similarly, in Colossians 1:17, Paul says of Christ that "in him all things hold together." The phrase "all things" refers to every created thing in the universe (see v. 16), and the verse affirms that Christ keeps all things existing—in him they continue to exist or "endure" (NASB, margin). Both verses indicate that if Christ were to cease his ongoing activity of sustaining all things in the universe, *then everything except the triune God would instantly cease to exist.*[4]

But the world keeps on existing and so do you.

So let's go with this definition for *providence*: "That which God creates He continually sustains and provides for, and nothing—great or small—is outside of His absolute control." He is the King and He has a plan. His sovereign plan for you and me and for the entire world will be worked out exactly according to His specifications.

When Joseph calmed his brothers' fears by asking them, "Am I in God's place?" he was looking backward over the events of his life. And when he looked backward over his life, he saw the sovereign providence of God that was directing his every step—even when he was kidnapped and sold into slavery.

When Joseph looked backward, he saw the perfect providential plan that had raised him to be co-king over Egypt. When he looked backward, he could see the remarkable organization of God's detailed plan for his life. God was in control of his life—even down to the tiniest details.

## Let's Break for Football

This might be getting a little heavy, so let's talk some football.

If you follow football you are familiar with Bill Belichick, the legendary coach of the New England Patriots. He has led the Patriots to three Super Bowl victories and is considered one of the greatest coaches in professional football today (despite the recent allegations of his spying on the practice sessions of upcoming opponents). But what you may not know is that his father, Steve Belichick, was probably the greatest scout in football history.

Steve Belichick was an assistant coach at Navy. His primary task was to scout the upcoming opponent and present a report to the coaching staff. Up until Steve Belichick, scouting was sort of a hit-or-miss operation. Steve Belichick turned it into a science.

Back in the fifties, college football was king; and Army and Navy were football powerhouses. In 1957, Army was loaded with two All-American running backs and an offense that rarely passed the ball. Steve Belichick had a philosophy of scouting: "Find out what the other guys do best—which is always what they want to do, especially under pressure in a big game—take it away from them, and make them do things they are uncomfortable with."[5]

Belichick spent hours figuring out what Army liked to do—and then he presented his plan to stop them to Navy Head Coach Eddie Erdelatz. It was the general consensus before a sold-out stadium that Navy had no chance of beating Army's powerful running offense.

But stop them they did.

Navy shut them down by making them do what they didn't want to do, which was to pass the ball. The Army team could never get on track and lost to Navy, 14-0.

In the locker room, a sportswriter congratulated Erdelatz on the win. Erdelatz pointed to Belichick and said, "He won the game for us two weeks ago."[6]

In other words, the scouting report that Steve Belichick turned in was so detailed and so exact that Navy won the game two weeks before they stepped onto the field.

You should know something about God.

God hasn't just scouted your future, He has planned your future.

And He didn't do it two weeks ago.

He did it before He created the worlds.

And that's why you are ultimately going to be a victor.

You don't have to be a victim. You may think that your life is over, as did Joseph as he headed off into a life of slavery. But because of God's great, eternal plan and His providential execution of that plan, Joseph became a victor.

And so will you—but like Joseph, you must come to grips with His sovereignty and providence. It's the only path out of victim-hood.

Jonathan Edwards said it best: "Every atom in the universe is managed by Christ so as to be most to the advantage of Christians."

That is a true and magnificent statement.

But it comes packaged with a warning.

A warning?

Why would we need a warning along with "every atom in the universe is managed by Christ so as to be most to the advantage of Christians"? Isn't that a statement that pretty much sums up the fact that we have a BIG GOD who works sovereignly and providentially in our lives?

Yes, it is. But with that statement is a biblical warning that you must factor into your life and your situation. Picture it as though you were reading it on a highway sign:

WARNING

GOD WORKS STRANGELY

GOD WORKS SLOWLY

## God Works Strangely

You now know the story of Joseph and his incredible ascent to co-ruler with Pharaoh.

But wasn't there an easier way to get him to the top?

If I were God and wanted to get Joseph up the ladder as the head man of Egypt, I would have planned for him to graduate from high school with the highest grades of anyone in his class. Then I'd work it so that he was also a great athlete. What a combination—a blue-chip athlete with a 4.0. And then I'd plan for Joseph to be named to the all-state football team, which would catch the eye of the football coach at the University of Egypt. Joseph would get a full ride to the school and major in business. But in the last game of his senior year he would blow out his knee—putting pro football out of the question.

Because of the setback in football, Joseph would go for an MBA and a PhD in public administration. Upon graduation, he would marry his high school sweetheart, step into a sweet government job, and after a stellar twenty-year career, would be handpicked by Pharaoh to oversee the coming agricultural crisis.

To me that makes a lot more sense. It would get Joseph to co-ruler status with a lot less difficulty and stress.

I've thought about it, and to me, it just seems like a better way.

But here's what God says about our "logical" ways and plans:

> "My thoughts are not your thoughts,
> Nor are your ways My ways," declares the LORD.
> "For as the heavens are higher than the earth,
> So are My ways higher than your ways
> And My thoughts than your thoughts."
> (Isa. 55:8–9)

His ways are not our ways. His thoughts are not our thoughts. His plans are not our plans.

*God works strangely.*

God's plan for Joseph included the evil that his brothers did to him. That's strange, isn't it? They had betrayed him and lied to their father. What they had done was a heinous and barbaric sin. Acting out of jealousy and sheer hatred, they intended it for evil.

But God intended it for good, to bring about this present result.

Do you see what Joseph is saying here? He is saying that the providence of God is bigger than anybody, anytime, anywhere. They intended it for evil, but God took their act of evil and intended it for good. He didn't stop it, and He didn't interrupt it. He let their evil plan come about. But all the time the invisible hand of our BIG GOD was in control of *every* detail and circumstance. When he was in the midst of it, Joseph was enveloped in shock, pain, and disbelief. But now, thirty-two years later as he looks backward, he sees the amazing providence of a good and holy God.

It's amazing—but it's also strange. Wonderfully strange.

## God Works Slowly

When he thought he was finished, when he thought all was lost, when his heart was broken with disappointment, even then the hand of his great God was working in his life. But it must have seemed that things would never change for Joseph. He had tasted the good life as head of Potiphar's household, but those days were long gone. He was in prison for a crime he didn't commit, and there was no hope for anything in his life to change. No big-shot lawyer to hire, no Supreme Court to whom he could appeal.

He was stuck. Finished. Day after day, week after week, month after month, he could see absolutely no prospect of life ever turning around. Nothing was happening! He was just maintaining, going about his business, trying to make the best of it.

Life was so mundane, so tedious, so *slow*.

But one call changed everything. And forty-five minutes later, he found himself the most powerful man on the face of the earth.

God works slowly.

God works strangely.

But God works.

And He knows precisely what He is doing with your life.

## Where We Are Going?

Here's the deal. In this book we're going to dive into the deep end. This is not going to be a Dr. Seuss, Cat-in-the-Hat kind of book. If that's what you're after, you'd better go back to the bookstore and find the kids' section.

If you're like me, you've probably wasted too much time in life's shallow end, walking around in the ankle-deep water and pretending you're swimming. I want to grow deeper and stronger as a man of God, and unless I miss my bet, I think you do too.

So get ready! We're going to dive deep into the life of this bold man of faith. And as we do, we will see ten undeniable evidences of the providence of God. These providences were true in Joseph's life and they are true in your life. Our chapter headings will simply declare the sovereignty and providence of our BIG GOD by stating ...

> HE IS IN CONTROL ...
> over devastating loss
> over all events
> over all assignments
> over all grievous setbacks
> over broken hopes
> over prolonged waiting
> over powerful people

over famine, weather, and disasters

over all promotion and advancement

over every event of your life, and will work it for good

You have a destiny and a work to do that God has foreordained for your life (Eph. 2:8–10). Nothing can stop it, and nothing can deter it. You may not see it or believe it or feel it as you read these words today, but no matter: He is in control.

When that fact dawned on David—perhaps out under the stars in the wilderness, watching his father's sheep—he sang these words:

In Your book were all written

The days that were ordained for me,

When as yet there was not one of them.

(Ps. 139:16)

Which is another way of saying it has been written, and it will come to pass.

Chapter Two

# When Your Dreams Die

## He Is in Control ...
## Over Devastating Loss

*"My times are in Your hand."*
*—David*

He was twenty-five, and it should have been the best year of his life. He married his sweetheart and carefully planned every detail of their honeymoon in Europe.

During an intense thunderstorm, however, his beautiful bride, Annie, was struck by lightning. As a result, she would be paralyzed for the rest of her life. For the next thirty-nine years, her husband faithfully took care of her. They were never able to travel again. Together they collected postcards from all over the world. They would never be able to see the beautiful sites in person, but together they enjoyed the pictures that friends would send to them on their travels.

The husband was the great Christian theologian Benjamin B. Warfield. For close to forty years, he taught his classes, wrote his articles, and took care of his wife. He was able to arrange his schedule so that he was rarely absent from her side for more than two hours at a time.

As a result of the paralysis, they were never able to have children or enjoy the life that they thought they would have together.

It was a devastating loss.

But to those who knew this couple best, they were not victims. Like Joseph, they were victors. Even in the midst of devastating loss.

Years later, it was Dr. Warfield who wrote these words concerning the providence of God. It's a lengthy quote, but I include it because of its profound wisdom. There's always a temptation to skim through books (I do it too, sometimes), but this quote is worth reading word for word. You've just read about Dr. Warfield's incredible loss. Now note the complete lack of bitterness or anger toward God in his words:

> Take any occurrence that happens, great or small—the fall of an empire or the fall of a sparrow, which our Lord himself tells us never once happens "without our Father." ... God is assuredly aware of everything that happens in his universe. There are no dark corners in it into which his all-seeing eye cannot pierce; there is nothing that occurs in it which is hidden from his universal glance. But certainly neither can it be imagined that anything which occurs in his universe takes him by surprise....
>
> Nor yet can he be imagined to be indifferent to its happening, as if, though he sees it coming, he does not care whether it happens or not. That is not the kind of God our God is; he is a God who infinitely cares, cares even about the smallest things. Did not our Saviour speak of the sparrows and the very hairs of our heads to teach us this?
>
> Well, then, can it be imagined that, though infinitely caring, God stands impotently over against the happenings in his universe, and cannot prevent them? Is he to be supposed to be watching from all eternity things which he does not wish to

happen, coming, coming, coming, ever coming, until at last they come—and he is unable to stop them?

Why, if he could not prevent their happening any other way he need not have made the universe; or he might have made it differently. There was nothing to require him to make this universe—or any other universe—except for his own good pleasure; and there is nothing to compel him to allow anything which he does not wish to happen, to occur in the universe which he has made for his own good pleasure.

Clearly things cannot occur in God's universe, the occurrence of which is displeasing to him. He does not stand helplessly by, while they occur against his wish. Whatever occurs has been foreseen by him from all eternity, and it succeeds in occurring only because its occurrence meets his wish.... We know that it could not occur unless it had a function to perform, such a place to fill, a part to play in God's comprehensive plan.

And knowing that, we are satisfied.[1]

It would not have been the plan of the newly married couple to encounter such tragedy on their honeymoon. Yet in the writings of this great Bible teacher, there is no seething rage at God. There is no sense that God needed to submit His plan to them for their approval. They are satisfied to simply trust and obey. Even in the midst of devastating loss.

The loss of health is devastating when it happens to someone who is young and full of life. But the loss of health is equally devastating as we come to our final years.

A famous man once uttered the words, "My life is over, but it is not yet ended."

In fact, Winston Churchill was eighty-five years old when he said those words to his daughter.[2] After suffering a series of minor strokes, the great British statesman sought to fight off depression, which he called "the black dog." Though his mind was still razor sharp, his body was beginning to shut down. He would live for another five years, but as far as he was concerned, his life was over—but not ended.

Joseph, son of Jacob, could have said those words at the age of seventeen.

"My life is over, but it is not yet ended."

Joseph's life was not over because he had lost his health. But in his mind he had lost something every bit as precious: his freedom.

Once Joseph became a slave, his life was over—but it was not yet ended.

## Into the Storm

It made absolutely no sense to this young man. How could the good God of Israel allow this to happen to him? His hopes, his dreams, and his ambitions were now gone—swept away in an instant. They were more than gone, they were dead and buried. His race was essentially over—and he had barely cleared the starting blocks.

Joseph couldn't have known it at the time, but this chapter of his life would last for *thirteen years*. During those years, at various intervals, he would be exhausted, humiliated, perplexed, and scared spitless.

At times, he had to wonder if he would survive. All his plans for life had fallen apart, utterly uprooted and demolished by the hateful actions of the very men who should have loved him and stood by him. His own brothers had plotted together to ruin his life.

But overshadowing the plan of his brothers was the plan of God.

Real and threatening, devastating and chaotic, the storms of life sometimes leave us wondering if we will even survive the day. Yet we do survive, to face the storm again the next day. Some storms are brief, flitting off our radar screens in a matter of hours or even minutes. A cloud passes in front of the sun, plunging the world into shadow, and then the sun shines through again, and life returns to normal.

Joseph's storm was thirteen years in duration.

And none of it made sense until he got through it.

Once he got through to the other side, he could look back over the events of those horrific years and see so clearly the well-ordered plan of almighty God. But when he was in that storm, it seemed like his life had spun completely out of control.

Perhaps that's the way you feel about your life right now. The needle is in the red zone, and events seem completely out of control. And if the truth were to be known, you agree with Churchill's evaluation of his life. That's right where you are.

My life is over—but it is not yet ended.

## Joseph's Devastating Loss

When Joseph was sold into slavery by his brothers, it was like the blow of a two by four right in the chops. No, much worse than that. A man might well recover from a blow to the face. But this? His life was over.

How do you think Joseph felt when he was on that camel? He wasn't stupid. He knew very well what happened to slaves. He knew he was finished. There was no way out of this deal. Who would rescue him? He would never see home or his family again. He had been viciously betrayed, and his life was ruined beyond repair.

Isn't that how you would have felt?

You've probably been through your own storms. Or perhaps your pain is not in the past tense, it's in the present. You're living right now in the shock of devastating loss. If that's true, then you have a pretty good handle on what Joseph was feeling on that camel ride to a life of slavery.

Maybe it never crossed this young man's mind at the moment, but in spite of all of the shock and pain Joseph was feeling, it was amazing that he was still alive. The brothers had fully intended to kill Joseph, and would have done so except for the fact that the providence of God stepped in—just in the nick of time.

There is a great old hymn with a title that speaks of God's providence: "Great Is Thy Faithfulness." I've always loved to sing that line "All I have needed Thy hand hath provided." The idea there is "All I have needed Thy hand hath *providenced.*"

What Joseph needed at that moment was for God to save him from being murdered. If the providence of God hadn't shown up at the exact right moment, he would have died. If God had been just fifteen seconds too late, it would have been too late to save him!

But that will never happen.

God is never early, and He is never late. He is always right on time. Sometimes we want Him to be early. And as you wait for Him, you see the clock ticking and begin to panic. But He will show up precisely at the right moment.

## Just in Time

Perhaps you've heard of "just-in-time inventory." It is a management and manufacturing technique often attributed to the late Edwards Deming. But Edwards Deming didn't come up with just-in-time inventory—God did. It's what you and I might call providence. He will always shows up in the nick of time and give you exactly what you need.

Elgin Staples was a nineteen-year-old sailor who served on the USS *Astoria,* a New Orleans–class heavy cruiser, in the Second World War. One morning, one of the large guns exploded and threw Staples overboard. He had shrapnel in both legs, and he was in shock. The only thing that kept his head above water was a lifebelt he was wearing at the time. When he hit the water, he was just conscious enough to trigger the button, inflating the device. The belt saved his life.

Four hours later, a passing destroyer plucked the young sailor out of the sea and returned him to his ship. Several hours after that, the captain decided to try to beach his ship, since the damage was much worse than he originally thought. The attempt to beach the ship, however, did not go according to plan, and incredibly, Elgin Staples found himself back in the ocean. He had never taken off the lifebelt that had saved his life, and it saved him again. Hours later he was rescued by another ship, the USS *Andrew Jackson*.

Lying on a bunk in sick bay, Staples never let go of the inflatable belt that had saved his life—twice. He studied every inch of its surface, noting its sturdy construction. Someone had very carefully put that belt together. Time and time again in that hospital bed, he would examine that belt and marvel that such a device could save his life twice in the same day. The irony was that the belt had been made in his own hometown of Akron, Ohio, at the Firestone Tire and Rubber Company.

After his hospitalization he was given an extended leave to go home and see his family. In his own words, he describes the homecoming:

> When I finally took my 30-day leave, I went home to my family in Ohio. After a quietly emotional welcome, I sat with my mother in our kitchen, telling her about my recent ordeal and hearing what had happened at home since I had gone away. My mother informed me that "to do her part," she had gotten a wartime job at the Firestone plant. Surprised, I jumped up and, grabbing my life belt from my duffel bag, put it on the table in front of her.
>
> "Take a look at that, Mom," I said. "It was made right here in Akron, at your plant."
>
> She leaned forward and, taking the rubber belt in her hands, she read the label. She had just heard the story and

knew that in the darkness of that terrible night, it was this one piece of rubber that had saved my life. When she looked up at me, her mouth and her eyes were open wide with surprise. "Son, I'm an inspector at Firestone. This is my inspector number," she said, her voice hardly above a whisper.

We stared at each other, too stunned to speak. Then I stood up, walked around the table and pulled her up from her chair. We held each other in a tight embrace, saying nothing. My mother was not a demonstrative woman, but the significance of this amazing coincidence overcame her usual reserve.

We hugged each other for a long, long time, feeling the bond between us. My mother had put her arms halfway around the world to save me.[3]

Did you notice that Mr. Staples referred to this event as an amazing coincidence? It wasn't coincidence—it was the goodness of God. It was providence. When something like that happens, you don't write it off to coincidence. *You give glory to God.* It was John Flavel who used to say, "Learn to adore providence." It always shows up just in time.

It was the providence of God that sent along the slave caravan at the exact moment when his brothers were pondering on how best to murder Joseph. Was he jumping up and down for joy that the slave caravan came along at just the right moment? Of course not—to him it was a crushing body blow. The worst possible scenario. But it was God's provision to actually save his life.

But he didn't know that, did he?

He figured his life was over. He would be a slave for the rest of his life. His life would be a living hell and a living death. Why would God allow such a terrible thing to take place?

Those thoughts had to be running through his mind as he attempted to absorb the crushing loss that had just occurred in his life. The providence of

God had saved him from death. But now that same providence was leading him into devastating loss.

Could it be true that God is behind devastating loss when it comes into our lives? Doesn't it make more sense to attribute these horrible losses to the attacks of the evil one?

As always, we must turn to the Scriptures for the answer.

## Waves of Loss

If you've ever lived near the ocean, you know that waves come in sets. Surfers sit on their boards with their backs to the beach, looking over the horizon for the next set. Waves come in sets of as little as three and as many as twelve or more. Then it's calm for several minutes and the next set rolls in.

In Psalm 88:7, a lonely psalmist wrote, "You have afflicted me with all Your waves." If you read the context, he's talking about hardship, suffering, and loss. It's not unusual for God to send difficulties to us in sets—and it's worth noting that they often seem to come in sets of threes.

Does it surprise you that the psalmist says that the Lord has afflicted him? He specifically says the waves are *God's* waves. The waves of difficulty breaking over him were from the Lord Himself. One of the great old sages of the faith, Thomas Watson, used to say that "whatever the affliction, it is the Lord who sends it."

Maybe you haven't thought about that before. But it's throughout your Bible. You may find yourself thinking, *That doesn't add up. Why would God send waves of affliction? That's pretty strange.*

Yes, it is strange.

But God works strangely.

We'll get back to Joseph and his devastating loss in a moment. But I want you to see that Job was in agreement with the psalmist when it came to the waves of suffering and devastating loss.

No one knew more about terrible loss than Job. In a period that was surely no more than a few minutes, three killer waves came out of nowhere, changing the landscape of his life forever. Each tsunami brought another devastating loss. It's important to note that Job was a man who was walking with the Lord, and had been enjoying the rich blessing of God upon his life. He was financially secure, he was a leader in the community, and he was deeply devoted to God.

He wanted his children to know the Lord as he did. He prayed for them and made sacrifices for them before the Lord.

This is the backdrop of Job's story. The curtain of heaven is pulled back, and we are given a ringside seat as Satan stands before God and throws a charge against Job. Satan's charge before the Lord is to the point: "Of course Job serves You and loves You! Who wouldn't? You've given him everything. He drives a Bentley, he vacations at his beach house in Maui, and his kids are perfect. Of course he's happy to serve You. And it isn't rocket science to see why."

The Lord then gives permission to Satan to afflict Job. But note that even though God grants permission to test Job, God remains in complete control of the process. Satan is not in control. *Satan had to ask for permission to prove his point.* That means that God is in absolute control. Satan didn't know it at the time, but his ploy would be used by God for thousands of years to declare His truth to countless generations.

## BIG GOD, Big Waves, Big Purposes

Our BIG GOD has purposes in mind here that Satan can't see or imagine. Even though God grants permission to Satan, HE IS STILL IN CONTROL.

> Now on the day when his sons and his daughters were eating and drinking wine in their oldest brother's house, a messenger came to Job and said, "The oxen were plowing and the

donkeys feeding beside them, and the Sabeans attacked and took them. They also slew the servants with the edge of the sword, and I alone have escaped to tell you." While he was still speaking, another also came and said, "The fire of God fell from heaven and burned up the sheep and the servants and consumed them, and I alone have escaped to tell you." While he was still speaking, another also came and said, "The Chaldeans formed three bands and made a raid on the camels and took them and slew the servants with the edge of the sword, and I alone have escaped to tell you." While he was still speaking, another also came and said, "Your sons and your daughters were eating and drinking wine in their oldest brother's house, and behold, a great wind came across the wilderness and struck the four corners of the house, and it fell on the young people and they died, and I alone have escaped to tell you." (Job 1:13–19)

In just five minutes or so, Job's life was ruined beyond repair. Did you notice the repeated phrase? *"While he was still speaking ..."* No sooner did Job absorb the shock of one piece of terrible news when he had to brace himself for the next.

In those few moments, Job's entire life as he knew it came to a halt. He lost his extensive livestock, his servants, and his children. He was wrecked economically and his servants had been killed—but then came the message that *all* of his children had been killed in a tragic disaster.

That's what you call devastating loss.

How would you react if this happened to you?

Scripture doesn't leave us to wonder how Job responded. The Bible says that he "arose and tore his robe and shaved his head, and he fell to the ground and worshiped. He said, 'Naked I came from my mother's womb, and naked I shall return there. The Lord gave and the Lord has taken away. Blessed be the

name of the LORD.' Through all this Job did not sin nor did he blame God"
(vv. 20–22).

If this happened to the average evangelical Christian today, here is what
he would say: "The Lord gave and Satan takes away, blessed be the name of
the Lord."

But please note that's *not* what Job said. He did not ascribe these tragedies
to Satan; he understood that the Lord was behind his devastating loss.

Thomas Watson ministered in London over three hundred years ago. Read
Watson's words carefully: "It is one heart-quieting consideration in all the afflictions that befall us, that God has a special hand in them: 'The Almighty hath
afflicted me.' Instruments can no more stir till God give them a commission,
than the axe can cut of itself without a hand. Job eyed God in his affliction:
therefore, as Augustine observes, he does not say, 'The Lord gave, and the devil
took away,' but 'The Lord hath taken away.'"

Watson was right when he said, "Whoever brings the affliction, it is God
that sends it." Satan could not have afflicted Job unless God granted him permission to afflict Job. So in reality, it was the Lord who afflicted Job. Satan was
simply the instrument of the affliction.

It was God who sent the waves of devastating loss crashing into Job's life.

## Another Wave

If there is any doubt about that at all, you should note Job's words in Job 2:8.
If you read the first seven verses of the chapter, you will see that the Lord had
another conversation with Satan about Job. God basically told Satan that he'd
been wrong about Job. Job's love for the Lord was still strong even though he
had suffered horrific loss. In essence, Satan responded by saying, "If You let me
take his health, I'll show You what's really in his heart!" The Lord then granted
permission for Satan to afflict Job physically.

Now here again we see the fact that God was always in complete control.

He granted permission once again to Satan to afflict Job physically. Understand this: God puts boundaries on what Satan can do. *Satan cannot go past the boundaries that have been set by the Lord.*

Satan afflicted Job with boils, sending the patriarch into absolute misery, with no relief in sight. His wife, who was a real winner, came to him with a discouraging word:

> Then his wife said to him, "Do you still hold fast your integrity? Curse God and die!"
>
> But he said to her, "You speak as one of the foolish women speaks. Shall we indeed accept good from God and not accept adversity?" In all this Job did not sin with his lips. (Job 2:9–10)

Now here is where so many of us go wrong. We think any good that comes our way is from the Lord, and anything hard and difficult comes from Satan. That's not what Job says! And it's not what the Scriptures teach. God is in control of the good pleasures in our lives, and He is in control of the adversity in our lives. He is in absolute control of everything.

The Lord sends the waves of blessing and the waves of loss.

The Lord gives and the Lord takes away.

Not Satan takes away—*the Lord* takes away!

Does this sound strange to you? It may sound strange because you have been watching too many preachers on Christian television. There are good teachers on Christian television and there are bad teachers. How do you tell the difference?

I would start with their hair.

If they have weird hair they tend to have weird doctrine. Funny how that works.

Thank the Lord that there are godly pastors who carefully explain God's Word through the medium of television. But there are other preachers who aren't so careful. All they preach is "prosperity." And if you are going to preach prosperity only, you've got a problem with the entire Bible. Prosperity preachers never preach Job. It gets in the way of their theology.

God is in control of prosperity, and He is in control of adversity, using both in the lives of His people. But most Christians have been taught that if devastating loss comes into your life, it must be from Satan.

This can be quite puzzling to us. Why would God allow devastating loss to come into our lives? If He controls everything, then why doesn't He stop the loss from occurring in the first place? If He could stop the tragedy that came into Job's life, then why in the world didn't He stop it?

There's a term that explains this strange working of God.

It's what you call a *cross providence.*


## Cross Providences

God has told us right up front that we're not going to understand Him. That's a biblical given. Earlier we looked at Isaiah 55:8, where the Lord tells us, "My thoughts are not your thoughts, nor are your ways My ways."

One of God's ways to accomplish His plan in your life is through the medium of cross providence. A cross providence is any event occurring in your life where it looks like God is working against you. A wave of affliction is a cross providence. A devastating loss is a cross providence. You know that you've been hit by a cross providence when you question the goodness of God in your life. To put it another way, a cross providence is a *deceptio visus.*

What the heck is a deceptio visus? (I didn't know either. I had to look it up). Deceptio visus is Latin for "visual deception." Thomas Fuller explains how it relates to the cross providences that happen in our lives:

> Take a straight stick, and put it into the water; then it will seem
> crooked. Why? Because we look upon it through two medi-

ums, air and water: there lies the deceptio visus; thus it is that
we cannot discern aright. Thus the proceedings of God, in
His justice, which in themselves are straight, without the least
obliquity [deviation], seem to us crooked: that wicked men
should prosper, and good men be afflicted … these are things
which make the best Christians stagger in their judgments.

And why? Because they look upon God's proceedings
through a double medium of flesh and spirit, so that all things
seem to go cross, though indeed they are right enough. And
hence it is that God's proceedings, in His justice, are not so
well discerned, the eyes of man alone not being competent
judges.[4]

There is more to what God is doing in cross providences than what our
eyes can see or our small minds can grapple with. But we don't understand His
ways, and we immediately think His ways are wrong. But they're not wrong—
they are right.

If God is in control, why didn't He just stop Joseph's brothers from selling
him into slavery? That was such a crushing loss for this young, idealistic man.

If God is in control, then why didn't He at least spare Job's children? One
daughter? One son? It seems so harsh and cruel that God would work in that way.

His ways are not our ways. But when God doesn't make sense, to borrow the title of James Dobson's outstanding book, there is something we can
count on even when we can't immediately see it. I'm speaking of the goodness
of God.

Psalm 119:68 declares that the Lord is good and does good.

At the moment you may not see the good. All you may see is the hurt,
pain, and wrenching grief of your loss. But the Lord is good and does good. At
the moment it may not *seem* good to us as we hyper-focus on our personal loss.
But in the purposes of God, in His way and in His time, and because He is in
control of all things, He will bring you to a point of seeing the good.

And consider this: *It may not even be on this earth that you see the good.* It was C. S. Lewis who speculated that when we die and find ourselves in heaven, the very first words out of our mouths will be "of course." What didn't make any sense on earth will immediately make sense in heaven. We eventually will see the good. Lewis was right about that, and he was no stranger to personal loss.

## What He Cannot Do

There are some things God cannot do.

He cannot lie.

He cannot sin.

He cannot do evil.

So the cross providences of life and the waves of life must be ultimately for our good.

God is holy. It is His primary attribute (Isa. 6). The holiness refers to His absolute moral purity. He cannot act against His nature. Because He is holy then He can only do good. He is good and does good—even when it doesn't look like it to us.

It didn't look like "good" to Joseph when he was headed to a life of slavery in Egypt. Where was the goodness of God in that? At the time, Joseph couldn't see it. But years later … he would.

## Bad Press

William Carey, considered the father of the modern missionary movement, sailed with his family to India in 1793 to preach the gospel. There was virtually no Christian witness at all in that massive nation. Carey's motto was "Expect great things from God, attempt great things for God."

He was soon joined by two friends, William Ward and Joshua Marshman. These three men threw themselves tirelessly into their work. By 1797, Carey had translated the entire New Testament into Bengali, and two years later, he was just two books shy of the entire Old Testament. In 1801, the Bengali New Testament came off the printing press. In those eight arduous years, Carey translated the New Testament into eight more Indian dialects.

And then came the fire. On March 11, 1812, a fire at the press destroyed valuable manuscripts, books, and type. The damage was estimated to be $50,000 (an unheard-of sum in those days).[5] And the translation work stopped dead in its tracks. Years of painstaking, difficult work vanished in a matter of minutes.

A devastating loss? You'd better believe it. And it sent shock waves across the ocean all the way to England. Touched by that tragedy, the churches began a fundraising drive. In six weeks, British Christians had raised enough money to replace the press.

As news continued to spread among the Christian community, more and more people became aware of Carey's work. As a result, more people than ever before wanted to financially support that pioneering missionary outreach, and others caught Carey's vision for spreading the gospel. As a result of the loss, more funds and more workers poured into India.

By the time of his death, Carey and his two friends, Ward and Marshman, had founded 26 churches and 126 schools (total enrollment: 10,000), translated Scripture into 44 languages, produced grammars and dictionaries, and organized India's first medical mission, savings bank, seminary, Indian girls' school, and vernacular newspaper.[6]

By the strange workings of a BIG GOD, the devastating loss had been turned into staggering gain.

> Behind our life the Weaver stands
> And works His wondrous will;
> We leave it all in His wise hands,

And trust His perfect skill.
Should mystery enshroud His plan,
And our short sight be dim,
We will not try the whole to scan,
But leave each thread to Him.[7]
—C. Murray

You may be thinking that God would never do that kind of thing for you. I think the Lord wants us to know that He does do those kinds of things on a regular basis. Everyone is different, and everyone has a different story. But God loves to take a huge setback and turn it into an astonishing victory or achievement.

God has a purpose and a plan for your life. He has done a good work in your life by bringing you to Christ. And He has also planned a work for you to do (Eph. 2:8–10). He had a work for Joseph to do that Joseph knew nothing about—and could not have imagined. And He has a work for you to do too.

When God starts a work, He finishes it. But don't take my word for it; it's an ironclad promise of Scripture: "He who began a good work in you will bring it to completion at the day of Jesus Christ" (Phil. 1:6 ESV).

God is in control of your devastating loss. He understands our hurts and broken hearts when we're blindsided. "The LORD is near to the brokenhearted and saves those who are crushed in spirit" (Ps. 34:18).

We shouldn't be surprised at the suffering and loss that come to us as we follow Christ. The Lord Jesus told us up front that "in the world you will have tribulation." Acts 14:22 tells us that "through many tribulations we must enter the kingdom of God." Philippians 1:29 clearly states the same truth: "It has been granted for Christ's sake, not only to believe in Him, but also to suffer for His sake."

Joseph experienced loss that staggered him. But his loss is an example for you and me. His loss was under the control of almighty God. So is your loss. And even when his loss made no sense at all to him, there was a smiling

Providence that was hidden behind the clouds of grief. His life wasn't out of control. It was under control.

God had something great in mind for him.

John Trapp said it best: "He that rides to be crowned, will not think much of a rainy day." Especially when he looks backward!

He could agree with Job when he cried:

> Oh that I knew where I might find Him,
> That I might come to His seat!
> I would present my case before Him
> And fill my mouth with arguments....
> Behold, I go forward but He is not there,
> And backward, but I cannot perceive Him;
> When He acts on the left, I cannot behold Him;
> He turns on the right, I cannot see Him.
> (Job 23:3–4, 8–9)

But then Job went on in the next verse and said something utterly astonishing: "But He knows the way I take; when He has tried me, I shall come forth as gold."

God doesn't waste this kind of suffering and loss. His plan for Joseph's life and Job's life was intentional and purposeful. And in both cases it involved great suffering and loss. But it wasn't random suffering. It was purposeful. God wouldn't leave them in their suffering. He was refining and testing both men, and one day they would both come forth as gold.

That was true for Joseph. It was true for Job. It was true for a young wife and her husband when a lightning strike brought devastating loss.

And it's true for you.

## Chapter Three

# Not a Chance

## He Is in Control ...
## Over All Events

*"The greatest single distinguishing feature of the power of God*
*is that our imagination gets lost thinking about it."*
—*Blaise Pascal*

Harold MacMillan was prime minister of Great Britain from 1957 to 1963. He was once asked by a young man what the greatest challenge he faced in being a statesman was.

"Events, my dear boy, events," MacMillan replied.[1]

Unforeseen events are a leader's greatest challenge.

It was wise old Thomas Watson who commented that "the godly man, when he dies, 'enters into peace' (Isa. 57:2); but while he lives, peace must enter into him." Knowing in your heart of hearts that our BIG GOD is in control of every event is the secret to finding a peace that can still your soul in the midst of an unsettling and unforeseen crisis.

A young navy pilot found that out one day as he went into battle. He was one of nine young American pilots who were shot down over the small island of Chichi Jima during World War II.

Eight of them were captured, tortured, beheaded, and cannibalized. Just one pilot escaped capture and survived. He was only twenty years old and scared to death. But he had a job to do, and he couldn't think about his fear. As he dove in to drop his bombs, scores of anti-aircraft guns zeroed in on his plane. Chichi Jima was a small island with two peaks that were the communication backbone of the Japanese Navy in the Pacific. The massive radio transmitters and antennas had to be preserved at all costs. That's why it was so heavily defended. And that's why the odds were against any pilot who would dive into that blistering hail of artillery fire.

As this young pilot was coming in to drop his bombs, his plane was hit. Somehow he managed to stay on course and drop the bombs. It took everything he had to pull the plane out of the dive and try to get away from the island. The damaged plane could not respond—it started to go into a downward spin. Over the intercom, he gave the command to his crew to bail out. Once they were out, he unbuckled and leaped out the door.

A parachute malfunction caused him to hit the water at a high rate of speed. He was four miles north of the island. Somehow, he managed to swim to a life raft that another plane had dropped.

But he was in big trouble.

There were no paddles, and the strong wind was blowing him into the island of torture and death. He was bleeding from the head, in great pain from the sting of a Portuguese man-of-war, and he was trying to get his bearings as he would periodically vomit over the side.

Once when he looked up, he saw the small boats from the island closing in on him to pick him up. He was completely defenseless. He knew that capture by the dreaded enemy was just minutes away.

It was then that he saw the strange object surface out of the ocean. He couldn't believe his eyes.

It was a periscope. And it was attached to an American submarine. Within minutes, he was onboard the *Finback* and safe from the enemy.[2]

Nine pilots were shot down. Eight were tortured, beheaded, and cannibalized. He was the only one to escape.

What unbelievable luck! What an incredible coincidence! What a stroke of fate!

Some would certainly say so. But they would be wrong.

That young navy pilot was plucked out of the sea by that sub because God had a work for him to do. His work was not done, and no enemy on earth could kill him until it was. That's why he wasn't killed and cannibalized like his buddies.

His name was George Herbert Walker Bush, and he would survive to become the forty-first president of the United States.

For the next sixteen weeks, that submarine was his home. He was assigned the watch from midnight to four a.m. when the sub was on the surface. In his own words, he describes the thoughts running through his young mind: "I'll never forget the beauty of the Pacific—the flying fish, the stark wonder of the sea, the waves breaking across the bow. It was absolutely dark in the middle of the Pacific; the nights were so clear and the stars so brilliant. It was wonderful and energizing, a time to talk with God.

"I had time to reflect, to … search for answers. People talk about a kind of foxhole Christianity, where you're in trouble and think you're going to die, and so you want to make everything right with God and everybody else right there in the last minute.

"But this was just the opposite of that. I had already faced death, and God had spared me. I had this very deep and profound gratitude and sense of wonder. Sometimes when there is a disaster, people will pray, 'Why me?' In an opposite way I had the same question: why had I been spared, and what did God have in store for me?"[3]

Joseph had to be asking the same question. His brothers had wanted to kill him, but the caravan of slavers had provided an escape from slavery. Yes, he was a slave, but at least he was alive. He must have been thinking—just as George Bush did on that sub—*Why have I been spared? What does God have in store for me?*

As you look back on your own life, can you remember a time when you had a brush with death? Did you walk away from a head-on collision when you were in high school, or did the lifeguard pull you out of the pool and get you breathing again?

That wasn't luck, and it wasn't a coincidence. *You are alive at this very moment because God still has a work for you to do.* The apostle Paul wrote, "For we are His workmanship, created in Christ Jesus for good works, which God prepared beforehand so that we would walk in them" (Eph. 2:10).

It's just that simple … and just that profound.

## Providence—Better Than Luck

Joseph was not sold into slavery because he was in "the wrong place at the wrong time." Thanks to the providence of God, he was actually in the *right* place at the *right* time—even though he would be sold into slavery. The betrayal of Joseph by his brothers was a critical factor and link in the will of God being accomplished in his life.

It wasn't that Joseph was having a bad day when they threw him into the pit. On that terrible day, Joseph was in the middle of God's will. How can that be?

In your life there is no luck, no chance, and no karma. There are no accidents and no random events. God is in control of every circumstance of your life. J. I. Packer sums it all up very nicely:

> The doctrine of Providence teaches Christians that they are never in the grip of blind forces (fortune, chance, luck, fate); all that happens to them is divinely planned, and each event comes as a new summons to trust, obey and rejoice, knowing that all is for one's spiritual and eternal good (Rom. 8:28).[4]

This immediately raises questions. Big questions. But if it is what the Scriptures say about God, then why we should we back away from it? The providence of God is one of the most reassuring doctrines in the entire Bible. It means that *nothing* can happen to you apart from God's plan for your life. We cannot forget Hebrews 1:3: "[Christ] upholds all things by the word of His power."

He is in control of *everything,* and that includes all circumstances in the universe. That would include the circumstances of Joseph's life … and your life as well.

But if He is in control of everything, then that has to raise at least two questions:

Is God the author of evil?

What about my will and my choices?

Well, what about evil? That's the first question that comes to mind. Evil certainly happened in Joseph's life. He did not sugarcoat the truth with his brothers: *"As for you, you meant evil against me.…"*

If God is in charge of everything in my life, and evil happens in my life, then isn't God responsible for evil? Doesn't that make Him the author of evil? The late great pastor and theologian Dr. Martyn Lloyd-Jones takes that question head-on:

> The great problem is this: if God does govern and control everything, then what is his relationship to sin? All I can do, in answer, is to lay down a number of propositions that are clearly taught in Scripture. The first is that sinful acts are under divine control, and occur only by God's permission and according to his ultimate purpose (Gen. 45:8).
>
> The second is that God restrains and controls sin (Ps. 76:10).
>
> The third is that God overrules sin for good (Gen. 50:20).
>
> My last proposition is that God never causes sin, nor approves of it; he only permits, directs, restrains, limits and overrules it. People alone are responsible for their sin (James 1:13–15).[5]

Proverbs 16:4 states,

> The LORD has made everything for its own purpose,
> Even the wicked for the day of evil.

It was Thomas Watson who observed, "The wisdom of God is seen in this, that the sins of men shall carry on God's work; yet that He should have no hand in their sin. The Lord permits sin, but does not approve it."

Could the Lord have stopped Joseph's brothers from doing evil and selling him to the slavers? Of course He could. In a heartbeat. But He didn't. He intended to use that evil to bring incomprehensible good to Joseph *and* his brothers.

But at that moment of great evil, Joseph had to be on the verge of absolute despair. His situation appeared to be utterly hopeless.

Here's an old poem about hopelessness from a man who knew about the sea. You and I may never experience this, but if you ever find yourself in a small ship in the midst of great, angry ocean, you will understand why it can drive a sane man nearly out of his mind. In the darkness, deafening noise, and violence of that scene, a man will experience utter hopelessness and despair.

Unless he knows the Lord.

> Away, Despair! My gracious Lord doth hear:
> Though winds and waves assault my keel,
> He doth preserve it: he doth steer,
> Ev'n when the boat seems most to reel:
> Storms are the triumph of his art:
> Well may he close his eyes, but not his heart.
> —Pastor George Herbert

## The Reality of Evil

Evil and sin are real, and at times in our lives it feels like they overwhelm everything else.

But they don't.

God is bigger than evil and sin. Evil will never get in the way of God's plan for your life. God is so big and so great that He makes evil cooperate and fold into His plan. He is sovereign, but we are responsible for our choices and decisions.

Here's what we can say about almighty God. He is in control, and His will is bigger than anyone's.

He is in control not only of *everything* but of *everyone*. That includes anti-aircraft projectiles and the men who pull the triggers. It includes jealous brothers and the scheduling of slave caravans. And it includes young wives hit by lightning on their honeymoons.

That's not easy to swallow. We don't see how that can be right.

Some things are beyond our comprehension. There are some reasons of God He has chosen not to reveal (Deut. 29:29). And in the meantime, we can only stand with Job when he declares, "Even though He slay me, yet will I trust Him."

It's easy to trust in a time of great favor and prosperity.

It's hard to trust in a time of shock and grief.

But we are called to do both.

## Strong Wills

Your four-year-old has a will. But that doesn't mean that you let your four-year-old run your family. Some of you do, and you'd better bring that to a halt immediately. Wise parents do not let the will of a four-year-old run and dominate the entire household.

God the Father has given us wills. But He has not turned over the direction of the universe to our wills and whims. He is in control of *every* circumstance that occurs in my life.

Several months ago I was walking through a casino in Las Vegas. I'd been invited to speak at a prayer breakfast being held in conjunction with a national convention of orthodontists. As I crossed through the casino and saw people throwing dice and placing their bets on the roulette wheel, I thought of Proverbs 16:33:

> The lot is cast into the lap,
> But its every decision is from the LORD.

Those people in Vegas who throw the dice are betting that chance will give them a payoff. But it's not chance that determines how the dice come up, it's the Lord. The Lord has predetermined the outcome *before* they throw the dice. He does that in every casino and in every back alley in the world where dice are being thrown.

How can that be?

Well, it's really very simple. He controls the dice, He controls the casino, and He controls Vegas. That's because He *owns* Vegas. That's why what you do in Vegas won't stay in Vegas.

He owns it all because He is in control.

Psalm 24:1 makes the case:

> The earth is the LORD's, and all it contains,
> The world, and those who dwell in it.

That verse doesn't say that the earth is the Lord's and most of what it contains. It doesn't say that the world belongs to the Lord and most of the people in it.

It says He owns it all. It also says that He rules over all. And if we go back to our doctrine of providence and Proverbs 16:33, it becomes very clear that He has *ordained* it all. By the way, *ordain* means "to establish or order by appointment or decree."

So let me get this straight.

He owns it all.

He rules over all.

He has ordained all.

He controls it all.

That means I shouldn't have trouble sleeping tonight.

Joseph knew that about God. That's why he could say to his brothers, "You meant evil against me, but God meant it for good in order to bring about this present result, to preserve many people alive" (Gen. 50:20).

When Joseph's brothers pulled him up out of that pit and sold him to the Midianite slave traders, it just wasn't the luck of the draw in operation that day. It was the sovereign plan of God at work.

He is in control over all the circumstances of your life, and that includes …

random events,

random crimes, and

random arrows.

## Random Events

Since God is in control over all circumstances that occur in your life, there really are no random events. The word *random* means "done, chosen, or occurring without a specific pattern, plan, or connection."

That will never happen in your life. Because of the plan and providence of God, *every* circumstance and experience of your life fits into God's pattern, plan, and purpose. Everything in your life is connected by the providence and power of God. Therefore, there are no random events. It all happens for a reason. But in most cases, we don't know what the reason is.

Cyrus Ahab was a left-handed pitcher for the Detroit Tigers. He may have been the most unlikely man in America to have ever pitched in the major leagues. When he was just a boy, he suffered a tragic accident with a hay baler that left him with a wooden leg, a glass eye, and a mangled left hand. But from 1913 to 1918, this incredible young man won over a hundred games with a wicked curveball that absolutely baffled batters.

The reason that Cyrus Ahab had such a phenomenal curveball was that he had only two fingers and a thumb on his left hand. As a result, he pitched the ball with an amazing rotation. Its sudden drop as it approached the plate rendered it virtually impossible to hit.

What finished his career was not his arm but his wooden leg. After years of strenuous work, the shortened limb finally couldn't bear Ahab's weight when he followed through after releasing the ball. And finally his childhood injuries brought his life in baseball to an end.

Nice story. But it's not true. I just made it up.

I pulled this story out of the air because I wanted to introduce you to two guys who really did exist in the Old Testament. They were both kings. One was named Cyrus and the other was named Ahab.

Neither one of them had much of a curveball. But both of them prove the point that there is no luck and there are no accidents in a person's life. Nothing was random in their lives. And nothing is random in yours.

Let's start with Cyrus, not a king of Israel but of Persia. His story is one of the most amazing in all the Bible. Over a hundred years before he was born, God spoke through the prophet Isaiah to Cyrus—calling him by name, and telling him what He was about to do. In Isaiah 44:28, God says, "It is I who says of Cyrus, 'He is My shepherd! And he will perform all My desire.'"

In plain English (and plain Hebrew before that), God comes right out and says, "I'm going to use a man named Cyrus to do My will and execute My plan." And everyone is looking at each other saying, "Cyrus? Who is Cyrus? Do you know anybody named Cyrus? Is he that new guy who moved in down the street?"

There was a simple reason people in that day didn't know about Cyrus. *He hadn't been born yet.* He wasn't even a gleam in his daddy's eye—or his grand-dad's eye for that matter. But what was really wild was what God said next about what Cyrus would do for Him.

> It is I who says of Cyrus, "He is My shepherd!
> And he will perform all My desire."
> And he declares of Jerusalem, "She will be built,"
> And of the temple, "Your foundation will be laid."

Now here is why this was strange.

At the time this was written, Jerusalem didn't *need* to be built. It was already built. And God's temple didn't need a foundation, because it already had a foundation. A good one.

But not for long. The nation of Judah was about to collapse and be destroyed by the king of Babylon, and many of its citizens would be carted off to Babylon as exiles. And Jerusalem? It would be a smoking ruin, without one stone left on top of another.

Those exiles in Babylon (including Daniel and his three friends) would be in captivity for seventy years. But then the combined armies of the Medes and the Persians would defeat mighty Babylon. In time, a king named Cyrus would arise with a novel idea: He would allow all the Jews, who were willing, to return to their homeland and their old capital, Jerusalem. He further decided that if he was going to let them go back home, he'd better help them rebuild their temple and their city from the ground up.

And that's what happened. Persian King Cyrus performed a mighty work that had been proposed by God (and recorded by the prophet Isaiah) decades before he was even born.

Cyrus did not know the Lord from his heart (Isa. 45:1–5), but he knew that God had commanded him to do a great work (2 Chron. 36:22–23).

This pagan king knew that there was nothing random about his life.

Do you know that about your life?

Theologian John Frame sets the context for us:

> Through the centuries of redemptive history, everything has come from God. He has planned and done it all. He has not merely set boundaries for creaturely action, but has actually made everything happen.
>
> Thus, God rules the whole course of human history.... But God does not control only the course of nature and the great events of history. As we have seen, he is also concerned with details. So we find in Scripture that God controls the course of each human life. How could it be otherwise? He controls the history of nations and human salvation. But these, in turn, govern to a large extent the events of our daily lives. Conversely, if God does not control a vast number of individual human lives, it is hard to imagine how he would be able to control the great developments of history.
>
> In fact, Scripture teaches explicitly that God controls the course of our individual lives. That control begins before we are conceived. God says to Jeremiah,
>
> "Before I formed you in the womb I knew you,
>
> Before you were born I set you apart;
>
> I appointed you as a prophet to the nations."
>
> (Jer. 1:5).[6]

It all had been planned before his birth. That was true for Joseph, it was true for Jeremiah, it was true for Cyrus, and it is true of you.

There is *nothing* in your life that is random. It's all part of the plan.

And nobody proves that point more than Ahab—the consensus favorite for the most evil king in the history of Israel.

## A Random Crime

The biblical account of King Ahab contains an incomparable illustration of the providence of God. The king's death, as foretold by the prophet Elijah, demonstrates the fact again that even apparent "random" events are part of God's providential plan.

So let me back up a little bit and give you a quick look at Ahab, one of the truly diabolical men in the Bible. In a long line of wicked kings of Israel, Ahab distinguished himself by being the worst. The Bible says of him, "Ahab … did more to provoke the LORD, the God of Israel, to anger than did all the kings of Israel before him" (1 Kings 16:33 NIV). I can't think of a more frightening designation than that. If you ever find words like that on your résumé, you need to do some serious repenting … *fast.*

Ahab lived in rebellion to the God of Israel all the days of his life. He was married to a foreign woman by the name of Jezebel, one of the most evil women to walk the face of the earth in all recorded history. This husband-and-wife political team thought they ruled over Israel and that they could get away with anything.

Instead of worshipping the Lord God, Jezebel influenced Ahab and the entire nation to worship Baal. This is why God sent Elijah to confront them in 1 Kings 16. Elijah told them that because they prayed to Baal to provide rain, God Himself would withhold the rain from the land for what would prove to be three and a half years.

Ahab and Jezebel hated Elijah, and they hated God. Read the biblical account, and you will see that this was one cold-blooded couple. In one instance, after Ahab coveted the vineyard of an Israelite named Naboth, Jezebel had the innocent man framed and murdered. When you think you're above the law, you imagine you can get away with anything, including murder. They did not see themselves as accountable to anyone, including God.

Now if you were living in Israel under a king like Ahab, and you feared the Lord, wouldn't you be thinking that things were "out of control"? Why would God allow a couple like this to occupy the throne of the nation? It was John Calvin who observed, "When God wants to judge a nation, he gives them wicked rulers." In other words, even when it seems that things are out of control, they are under control.

God sent His servant Elijah to deliver a message to Ahab.

> Then the word of the LORD came to Elijah the Tishbite, saying, "Arise, go down to meet Ahab king of Israel, who is in Samaria; behold, he is in the vineyard of Naboth where he has gone down to take possession of it. You shall speak to him, saying, 'Thus says the LORD, "Have you murdered and also taken possession?"' And you shall speak to him, saying, 'Thus says the LORD, "In the place where the dogs licked up the blood of Naboth the dogs will lick up your blood."'" (1 Kings 21:17–19)

Don't miss the providence of God over *all* circumstances in this story. Elijah tells Ahab that his own blood would be licked up by the dogs in the very same place where Jezebel killed Naboth. Only God could predict what would happen and then pull it off. It takes great power to pull off such a prophecy. It takes absolute control over all circumstances to make that happen. But that's not a problem for the Lord.

By the way, the Lord had a message for Jezebel that Elijah delivered in verse 23: Her blood, too, would be licked up by the dogs—within the walls of the city of Jezreel. That would be fulfilled to the letter as you can read for yourself in 2 Kings 9:30–37. Once again, God is in control of all circumstances. He makes no idle threats and He makes no empty promises. The king and queen's "random crime" was about to get a very specific piece of justice from a BIG GOD.

## A Random Arrow

Now let's get back to Ahab. He knew from his gut that the Lord was God, but he just couldn't bring himself to obey Him and serve Him. He believed the word of the Lord that came through Elijah. And for a very brief time, he actually humbled himself before the Lord (1 Kings 21:27–29). But it was more of a head fake than a genuine brokenness before God. It wasn't the real deal from the heart.

So instead of truly repenting and turning to the Lord for the long term, he quickly returned to his deceptive ways. Ahab talked Jehoshaphat (don't you love these names?), the king of Judah, into going to battle with him (1 Kings 22). Jehoshaphat, generally speaking, was a pretty good king.

But good king or not, this was a pretty stupid move.

It gets worse! Ahab suggested that Jehoshaphat wear his royal robes into battle, while Ahab would disguise himself. Ahab figured that the enemy would try to kill both of them as kings, and if he could paint a target on Jehoshaphat and camouflage himself, he would be safe. For some cockeyed reason, Jehoshaphat agreed to this.

Ahab, the lawless king of Israel, thought he could outmaneuver the providence of God by his cleverness. He found out that he could not.

> So the king of Israel and Jehoshaphat the king of Judah went up to Ramoth-gilead. And the king of Israel said to Jehoshaphat, "I will disguise myself and go into battle, but you wear your robes." And the king of Israel disguised himself and went into battle. Now the king of Syria had commanded the thirty-two captains of his chariots, "Fight with neither small nor great, but only with the king of Israel." And when the captains of the chariots saw Jehoshaphat, they said, "It is surely the king of Israel." So they turned to fight against him. And Jehoshaphat cried out. And when the captains

of the chariots saw that it was not the king of Israel, they turned back from pursuing him.

But a certain man drew his bow at random and struck the king of Israel between the scale armor and the breastplate. Therefore he said to the driver of his chariot, "Turn around and carry me out of the battle, for I am wounded." And the battle continued that day, and the king was propped up in his chariot facing the Syrians, until at evening he died. And the blood of the wound flowed into the bottom of the chariot. And about sunset a cry went through the army, "Every man to his city, and every man to his country!"

So the king died, and was brought to Samaria. And they buried the king in Samaria. And they washed the chariot by the pool of Samaria, and the dogs licked up his blood, and the prostitutes washed themselves in it, according to the word of the LORD that he had spoken. (1 Kings 22:29–38 ESV)

Did you notice how it was Ahab who was wounded? A certain man drew his bow at *random,* and the arrow just happened to find the one-inch seam between the scale armor and the breastplate that Ahab was wearing.

Now this is classic. Not only was Ahab disguised, but he was wearing body armor. He must have thought to himself, *Why would they come after me, now that I've talked Jehoshaphat into wearing the kingly robes?*

Just in case, as a backup plan, he put on the full suit of armor, including the breastplate. And he must have been riding in a Hummer chariot.

But some enemy soldier fired his bow at random. He didn't have a target and he didn't have a plan. *I shot an arrow into the air, it fell to earth I know not where....* He wasn't aiming at Ahab. He just set up an arrow in the bow and let her fly. And the most amazing thing happened with this random arrow. It somehow managed to find its way into a miniscule, unprotected seam between the armor and the breastplate that Ahab had so carefully put in place.

And that night, the dogs licked up the blood of Ahab in the very place where they had licked the blood of Naboth. In this way, the prophecy of Elijah was fulfilled, with all T's crossed and all I's dotted.

Only a God who is in control of all circumstances can pull that off.

Hebrews 9:27 says that "it is appointed for men to die once and after this comes judgment." This was Ahab's appointed time.

We all have an appointed time. The times of your death and my death have already been set from before the foundations of the world.

> Your eyes have seen my unformed substance;
> And in Your book were all written
> The days that were ordained for me,
> When as yet there was not one of them.
> (Ps. 139:16)

Before the brand-new planet earth took the first spin on its axis, God determined the moment of your conception, the moment of your birth, and the moment of your death. That's the clear teaching of Job 14:1, 5:

> Man, who is born of woman,
> Is short-lived and full of turmoil....
> Since his days are determined,
> The number of his months is with You;
> And his limits You have set so that he cannot pass.

What does this mean? It means "we are His workmanship, created in Christ Jesus for good works, which God prepared beforehand so that we might walk in them" (Eph. 2:10). God has planned out a work for you to do—just as He did for Cyrus and Joseph.

It means that *you cannot die until God's purposes for you on earth are accomplished.* And on the other hand, only a God who is in control of all circumstances can keep you alive when the bullets are flying.

## Last Words

Let's end with a final thought from Joseph's life. The original intention of Joseph's brothers was not to sell him, but to kill him (Gen. 37:18–28). But they didn't. God had a purpose for Joseph to fulfill—therefore he *couldn't* die.

When Joseph looked back on the events of his life, he remembered that his brothers wanted to kill him before they decided to sell him. But they didn't, and they didn't kill him for one reason.

God had a work for Joseph to do.

God had a work for George Bush to do.

The thousands of bullets didn't kill young George Bush. The jealous brothers didn't kill young Joseph. In each case, God intervened to keep these men alive. Only a God who is in control of every circumstance of your life can pull that off.

They might rough you up.

They might talk about you behind your back.

But as George Whitefield used to say, "I cannot die until my work is done."

And neither can you.

## Chapter Four

# Take This Job and Shovel It

## He Is in Control ...
## Over All Assignments

*"The hardness of God is kinder than the softness of men."*
—C. S. Lewis

You may remember the old country song "Take This Job and Shove It."

Here's another option: Take your job and shovel it under the providential and strange plan that God is working out in your life.

What is your current assignment in life?

Are you pleased with it? Do you hate it? Or do you feel that you're just drifting right now, without any assignment that you can discern? Some assignments are welcomed and some are unwanted.

*But they are all from the Lord.*

Psalm 37:23 is very clear: "The steps of a man are established by the LORD." God is in control of your journey and of your destination ... *right now.* And He is in control over the assignments of life.

It is God Himself who assigns us to our posts. When God gives you such an assignment, it doesn't necessarily mean you'll be there forever. It could all change in a year or in a month or in a week. It could change tomorrow.

But you're there for now.

You may be bored, you may be overqualified, you may be unchallenged, you may sense you are unwanted, and you may feel like a fish out of water. But that doesn't mean that the assignment is a waste. The Lord doesn't waste our lives. He knows precisely what He is doing when He gives us our assignments.

So let's say you're in an assignment right now that's not to your liking. You're not sure how you got there, and you certainly don't want to stay there. But don't become so upset or discouraged that you miss one very important fact: Most likely, that assignment you're in isn't final. But it is somehow preparing you for the work God has for you to do.

In God's plan, there are no wasted assignments.

In God's plan, every assignment is preparation.


## Slave in the Big House

Joseph was now a slave in the house of Potiphar. In this new and unwanted assignment, the Lord had not forgotten Joseph. On the contrary, Joseph's assignment as a slave in Egypt was a necessary and critical part of the strange and wonderful work that God had for Joseph to do.

F. B. Meyer paints the picture of what Joseph must have experienced when he arrived in Egypt for a life of slavery:

> In some great slave market he was exposed for sale, together
> with hundreds more, who had been captured by force or stealth
> from the surrounding countries. He was bought by Potiphar,
> the "captain of the guard," who was, in all likelihood, the chief
> of the royal bodyguard, in the precincts of the court.... Potiphar
> was an Egyptian grandee; a member of the proud aristocracy;
> high in office and in court favor. He would no doubt live in a

splendid palace, covered with hieroglyphs and filled with slaves. The young captive [Joseph] must have trembled as he passed up the pillared avenue, through sphinx-guarded gates, into the recesses of the vast Egyptian palace where they spoke a language of which he could not understand a word, and where all was so new and strange.[1]

If you had told Joseph as he entered through those doors that one day he would be completely in charge of this vast palace and its operations, he would have said, "You're out of your cotton-pickin' mind." But that's exactly what God—the God who controls everything—had in mind for him. As far as Joseph was concerned, he was at rock bottom in life.

I recently read a biography of another man who, at a rather late place in life, hit absolute rock bottom. At the age of fifty-one, he considered himself to be a failure with virtually no future ahead of him.

His name was Dwight Eisenhower and little did he know what was in store for him. But at fifty-one, he couldn't see any of it. Here is how Stephen Ambrose described the life of Eisenhower, the Allied supreme commander of World War II and thirty-fourth president of the United States:

Eisenhower was one of the outstanding leaders of the Western world of this century. As a soldier he was professionally competent, well versed in the history of war along with modern strategy, tactics, and weaponry, decisive, disciplined, courageous, dedicated, popular with his men, his superiors, and his subordinates.

As president, he was a leader who made peace in Korea and kept the peace thereafter, a statesman who safely guided the free world through one of the most dangerous decades of the Cold War, and a politician who captured and kept the confidence of the American people. He was the only president of the twentieth century who managed to preside over eight years of peace and prosperity.[2]

Again, at age fifty-one, Eisenhower could see none of that future success. Ambrose sums up Eisenhower's dismal situation:

> He had given his life and talents to the army. He was fifty-one years old; only the coming of war had saved him from a life of forced retirement and a life with no savings and but a small pension to live on. Although he had impressed every superior for whom he had worked, he had no accomplishments to his credit that he could point to with pride for his grandchildren. Had he died in 1941, at an age when most great men have their monumental assignments behind them, he would be completely unknown today.[3]

The Lord had much more in mind for Dwight Eisenhower than he could've possibly known. And the same was true for Joseph when he was assigned to become a slave in Potiphar's great estate. Joseph was at rock bottom, but in God's mind, Joseph's assignment was just a necessary stepping-stone to the next assignment. Although the young man couldn't have known it, he had an appointment with success awaiting him.

Now, what was God's ultimate work for Joseph going to be?

One day in the not-so-distant future, he would run and administrate the great nation of Egypt in a time of monumental prosperity, in preparation for a great national crisis.

Did Joseph know that? No. Joseph had never read Genesis. He didn't know his Bible, because the Bible didn't exist. So how in the world would he be trained to run a large nation? By first learning how to run a large household—Potiphar's household. Because Potiphar was a high-ranking official in Pharaoh's inner circle, he didn't live in a normal house. He lived in a great palace on a huge estate, with a large infrastructure of servants and employees to keep it going.

That was Joseph's first semester in kingdom administration. In his next semester, he would learn how to run a large jail.

Then he would be ready to run a large nation.

Now let me see if I can get this progression straight: large estate ... large jail ... large nation. Sounds like a plan, doesn't it?

Here's the point. *None of the assignments in Joseph's life were wasted.* They were all part of the plan that he couldn't see. And the same goes for you. God is in control of everything. Therefore, three observations concerning our assignments will give us a glimpse into how the providence of God often works:

*Sometimes God will give you a dead-end assignment.*

*Sometimes there will be an assignment within an assignment.*

*Sometimes God will refuse your desired assignment.*

## A Dead-end Assignment

Joseph had a new assignment. He was going to be a slave. It wasn't what he wanted, it wasn't what he expected, and it wasn't what he had dreamed of as a young man in his father's house.

But it was a fact.

His assignment in life, as far as he knew, was that of a slave for the rest of his life. Genesis 39:1 fills in the details:

> Now Joseph had been taken down to Egypt; and Potiphar, an Egyptian officer of Pharaoh, the captain of the bodyguard, bought him from the Ishmaelites, who had taken him down there.

Let's face it, sometimes in life, we hit a dead end. We think we're following a star and we end up in a ditch ... or in a slum ... or in a blind alley. There are dead-end places and there are dead-end jobs. The problem with a dead-end place is that there is no way out. That's exactly where Joseph was—he was a slave and he would always be a slave. Slaves don't have a lot of options. As a matter of fact, they don't have any.

Perhaps you are in a dead-end place or in a dead-end assignment.

So how did you get there?

Ultimately, the Lord put you there. And He has put you there for a reason. *What reason?* you ask. For now, the answer to that question is hidden from you. It's a secret known only to the Lord (Deut. 29:29).

People in dead-end places or in dead-end assignments tend to think they will be there forever. But you won't. In fact, God has you in a place of preparation, and those dead-end places are very critical to what God plans to ultimately do in your life. God uses dead-end assignments to get you ready for what He has planned for you in the future. But so often in those dark, discouraging places, we think we have no future.

This is what happened to Dwight Eisenhower. I want to go back to his life because so little is known about his story. But along with Winston Churchill, he was the key leader of World War II. He was the General of Generals—over Patton, Montgomery, Bradford, and the whole lot of them. He was the one who developed the strategy for D-Day. But very little, relatively speaking, has been written about his life. I have numerous biographies of Churchill, but only two on Eisenhower. But his story is nearly as remarkable as Churchill's.

Why did Eisenhower wonder at fifty-one if he had any significant future? "He had been in the army since 1911. During the past twenty-nine years, he had been consistently praised by his superiors and classed in the top category for his age and rank. He had attended the army's leading postgraduate schools and graduated first at the Command and General Staff school. But nothing that he had done had had the slightest influence in pushing him ahead.… No matter how good an officer was, no matter how well he did his duty, his promotion was governed strictly by the rules of seniority.

"On one occasion, Eisenhower told his son, John, that in the business world a man could go as far as his character, abilities, and honorable ambitions would carry him. But in the army, things are ordered somewhat differently."[4]

Seniority governed all promotions until a man became a colonel, but in sixteen years, Eisenhower had received just one promotion, and he was only a major. With his age, he couldn't see any way that he would make it to colonel. And if he ever did, he would be so close to compulsory retirement that he would never achieve the rank of general.

Here was a brilliant and gifted leader—full of energy and on fire to do something with his life. But he was stuck. That's why he was discouraged and at rock bottom.

The great general Douglas MacArthur in the early 1930s had said of Eisenhower, "This is the best officer in the army."[5] MacArthur said those words when Eisenhower was a captain. But the "best officer in the army," no matter what he did, could not get ahead.

MacArthur's statement was not flattery. He meant every word. MacArthur had chosen Eisenhower to be his chief of staff in 1929, so he knew firsthand what Eisenhower could do. And here was one of the reasons that Eisenhower couldn't get ahead—MacArthur wouldn't let him go anywhere else. So for ten years, Eisenhower labored under the shadow of the general with the huge ego, Douglas MacArthur. Eisenhower wanted to see more action, but every time he would request a transfer, MacArthur would turn him down. No matter what he did, he could not seem to get ahead. He was bored to tears doing details for the general. But he couldn't catch a break to get out and show his leadership ability.

MacArthur even admitted to holding him back in a letter of commendation that he sent to Eisenhower in 1935:

> The number of personal requests for your services brought
> to me by heads of many of the army's principal activities
> during the past few years furnish convincing proof of the
> reputation you have established as an outstanding soldier. I

can say no more than this reputation coincides exactly with my own judgment.[6]

For ten years Eisenhower labored under MacArthur, the last five in the Philippines. In his own heart, he felt that he was at a dead end.

Eisenhower was in a dead-end assignment, as was Joseph. And perhaps you are too.


## No Dead End Is Permanent

Every dead-end place and dead-end assignment has a beginning, a middle, and an end. God has set borders around your dead-end place. He has lessons for you to learn in the dead-end place that can be learned nowhere else. Your dead-end place will probably have a midterm and a final, along with a number of quizzes along the way. God has set the dates of the semester. It has a beginning and it has an end. But you have no idea what those dates are.

The longer you are in a dead-end place, the more convinced you become that you will always be there. You begin to think there's no way out. But at the right time, there will be.

I have a friend who oversees the editorial and biblical content of numerous Christian books that are published each year—books published in many languages and distributed all over the world. Overseeing a large contingent of authors, he makes critical decisions about biblical content and doctrine. It's his job to make sure that truth is kept in balance. His position is a critical one that affects the lives of potentially millions of people.

He was a top student in seminary, taking his course work very seriously. Graduating with honors, he fully expected God to enrich his ministry. But after pastoring a church for just a few years, he was asked to leave. Devastated, my friend began to look for another ministry position. But no matter how diligently he searched, there was nothing. For three years the only job he could get was delivering newspapers.

That was it.

Every morning he would be up at four, throwing newspapers. It was a dead-end job in a dead-end place. At times he thought he would be there forever. He thought God had passed him by.

When my friend was throwing papers, he felt like a failure. But the Lord was with him, and he was on his way to becoming a successful man.

When you find yourself in a dead-end assignment, you are not alone. It may feel like you're alone, but you're not. Joseph was a slave in a foreign nation with a foreign culture and a foreign language. He didn't know a soul, and he was completely cut off from friends and family. But the Bible makes it clear that he wasn't alone. Genesis 39:2 declares a significant truth:

*The Lord was with Joseph.*

Here's the context of that statement:

> Now Joseph had been taken down to Egypt; and Potiphar, an Egyptian officer of Pharaoh, the captain of the bodyguard, bought him from the Ishmaelites, who had taken him down there. The LORD was with Joseph, so he became a successful man. And he was in the house of his master, the Egyptian. Now his master saw that the LORD was with him and how the LORD caused all that he did to prosper in his hand. So Joseph found favor in his sight and became his personal servant; and he made him overseer of his house, and all that he owned he put in his charge. It came about that from the time he made him overseer in his house and over all that he owned, the LORD blessed the Egyptian's house on account of Joseph; thus the LORD's blessing was upon all that he owned, in the house and in the field. So he left everything he owned in Joseph's charge; and with him

there he did not concern himself with anything except the food which he ate. (vv. 1–6)

*The Lord was with Joseph, so he became a successful man.*

On the face of it, that statement is absurd. Slaves don't become successful men. Slaves don't win friends and influence people. But Joseph did. He became a successful man for one reason: The Lord was with him. And it was so clear that the Lord was with him that even Potiphar, a hard-shelled Egyptian politician and insider, could see it.

Joseph's initial assignment may have been the worst of the worst. And yet the Lord was with him in that assignment. And if the Lord is with you, all bets are off. Everything changes. Anything becomes possible.

If the Lord is with you—no matter what dead-end situation you find yourself in—everything is eventually going to be fine. It may not be fine right now, but one day things will come together for your greater good. Eventually Potiphar was so impressed that he made Joseph overseer of his house. Joseph handled everything for him—just like Eisenhower did for MacArthur. All Potiphar had to do was to decide if he wanted a cheeseburger or lasagna for dinner.

Joseph had done very well. He was a successful man in a dead-end assignment because the Lord was with him.

But there is more to the story than his external success.

## An Assignment Within an Assignment

The text doesn't say that the Lord was with Joseph and he *instantly* became a successful man. It says he *became* a successful man. In other words, this all didn't happen in twenty-four hours. God was taking him through a very critical and necessary process. God is usually working on more than one front in our lives. He has multiple purposes that we absolutely cannot see. That's why sometimes there is an assignment within an assignment.

The first assignment was to be a slave.

The second assignment was to learn to forgive those who had sold him into slavery. A case could be made that the first assignment would be easier than the second. When you have been deeply wounded by someone, there is nothing tougher than learning to forgive.

As we have seen, the Lord gave Joseph *external* success. Or we could say he was given an obvious success, a clear success, or a noticeable success. But there was another kind of success that Joseph needed to develop.

This would be an *internal* success.

There was a process involved, and it didn't happen overnight. It didn't take weeks, and it didn't take months. It took years. Does the text say that? No, it doesn't. But if someone tried to murder you and then sold you into slavery, would you be able to forgive him in your heart and have the issue completely resolved over the weekend? Of course you wouldn't. And neither did Joseph.

*But he got over it.*

How?

By realizing that his BIG GOD was in control of his past, his present, and his future. At some point, Joseph began to trust God with his entire life. Did someone do evil to him in the past? Yes. Would someone else try to take him down in the future? Probably.

But no matter what evil someone does to us—past, present, or future—our God intends it for our good. That is absolutely mind blowing. And that truth is what enables you to forgive.

You don't have to become best friends with the person who took you down. But you don't have to hate his or her guts either. When you forgive, you can actually pray for the person and ask God to do good things in his or her life as well.

That's the lesson we all have to learn and keep on learning.

But it sure beats the heck out of being bitter.

So why don't you nick your own arm, suck out the poisonous venom of bitterness, spit it on the ground, and grind it deep into the dirt before it kills you. And then trust God to make your life sweet in His way and in His time.

I'm talking sweet like sweet tea in the South (that's iced tea with four cups of sugar to every cup of tea). But before you can enjoy that kind of sweetness, you've got to get rid of the venom.

Jesus has forgiven you.

There's not a reason in the world you shouldn't forgive someone else. I'm not saying it's easy. But the Lord made it very clear that it is necessary: "… forgiving each other, whoever has a complaint against anyone; just as the Lord forgave you, so also should you" (Col. 3:13).

Johannes Gutenberg was the man who invented the printing press. The first book that came off Gutenberg's press was the Bible. But although Gutenberg made sure that the Bible was the first book ever printed, he personally never got the message of the Bible. A case could be made that Johannes Gutenberg's invention of the printing press was the single most significant invention in history. That one invention dramatically changed the world. And when we think of this invention, we think of Gutenberg. But in his day, when people heard about the printing press, they didn't give credit to Gutenberg—they had never heard of Gutenberg.

All of the credit in Gutenberg's time for his invention didn't go to him. It went to Johann Fust. When Gutenberg came up with the idea and plan for the printing press, he didn't have the money to produce it. So he went to Fust and borrowed the money. It was an enormously expensive project to put the first printing press together. Later, Gutenberg went back to Fust and borrowed more money. As Gutenberg was just about finished perfecting his invention and ready to put out the first mass copies of the Bible, Fust took him to court.

The judge ruled in favor of Fust. Gutenberg lost his press, his ideas, his years of work, and even his tools. He was just days away from success, and he lost everything. When the Bible was printed, people marveled at the clarity of the letters and the beauty of the artwork. And they all were talking about Fust and his great invention.

Fust didn't even know how to put a sheet of paper into the press. Yet he was the one who was being praised as the inventor of the machine that was revolutionizing the world.

Gutenberg watched as everything was taken from him, including the credit for his invention. He never received a penny from his work of a lifetime. He died in poverty—a broken and bitter man.

To his dying day, he could never forgive Fust for his betrayal. And the poison of bitterness sapped every ounce of Gutenberg's energy and will to work.

It had been Gutenberg's dream to print the Bible. But he never understood the message of the Bible. The Bible is not a book about bitterness; it is a book about forgiveness.

## A Nagging Conscience

So why do we refer today to the first printed Bible as the Gutenberg Bible? Years after Gutenberg died, Fust's conscience kept hounding him. He couldn't live with himself. He was being granted praise and acclaim that belonged to another man. Finally, Fust came clean and gave the rightful credit for the printing press to Gutenberg. But Gutenberg was in his grave. And it was his own bitterness that had put him there.

Joseph became a successful man, and one of the reasons for that success was his decision to give his bitterness and hatred to the Lord and trust in the goodness of God.

Psalm 37:3 directs our attention to where our focus must be when we have been wronged:

> Trust in the LORD and do good;
> Dwell in the land and feed on His faithfulness.
> (NASB, margin)

Joseph's responsibility was to not stress out over his brothers and what they had done to him. He had to move on with his life. His trust was to be in the Lord.

When we are wasting the days of our lives in bitterness and anger over those who have wounded us, we are not trusting in the Lord and doing good. When our focus is continually on those who brought great pain to us, we are looking at life cross-eyed. We aren't seeing clearly, and we aren't trusting the Lord for our futures. Faith in the promise of God—that He will be faithful to us—looks through a more powerful lens that gives greater clarity to our circumstances. And as a result, we can move ahead, trusting God to make a way for us.

We are to dwell in the land, work at our given assignments, and feed on the faithfulness of God. The Lord knows exactly where you are, and He knows what has happened to you. But He has bigger plans for you, according to Psalm 37:4–5:

> Delight yourself in the LORD,
> And He will give you the desires of your heart.
> Commit your way to the LORD,
> Trust also in Him, and He will do it.

Have you ever gone to a counselor and been disappointed with the advice? You think to yourself, *I've wasted my time. I could have got better counsel than that from the UPS guy.* Well, here's some counsel that comes wrapped in a few verses of priceless wisdom. If you have been deeply wounded, if you have been betrayed, if you have been abused, if you have been robbed of wealth or reputation—this wise counsel is for you.

> Thy way, not mine, O Lord,
> However dark it be;
> O lead me by Thine own right hand
> Choose out the path for me.

Smooth let it be or rough,
It will be still the best;
Winding or straight, it matters not,
It leads me to Thy rest.

I dare not choose my lot;
I would not if I might;
But choose Thou for me, O my God,
So shall I walk aright.

Take Thou my cup, and it
With joy and sorrow fill;
As ever best to Thee may seem,
Choose Thou my good and ill.[7]

I believe this is what Joseph did. And it all began with forgiving his brothers instead of hating them.

There is nothing in the text that tells us of the process that Joseph went through in order to overcome his deep resentment, but he was human! He had to have had resentment. Joseph wasn't Superman. He was just a regular guy whose life had been destroyed. Of course he had to deal with this. And because it was a such deep wound, God would not allow it to fester. The longer the issue was ignored, the greater the chance for spiritual infection of the soul and heart.

God had great plans for Joseph. But He wouldn't promote him if he had a diseased heart and a bitter spirit. So this is where there had to be an assignment within an assignment.

Corrie ten Boom, along with her sister, spent many months in a Nazi concentration camp. Her sister was horribly abused and eventually died. Much of Corrie's ministry after the war was to survivors of the camps. On one occasion, Corrie made a telling statement about the survivors: "Those who were able to forgive their former enemies were able to return to the outside world and rebuild their lives—those who nursed their bitterness remained invalids."

Corrie ten Boom personally forgave one of the most brutal guards in the camp who killed her sister. She moved on to a productive life because she learned to forgive.

Joseph went through the same process. By forgiving his brothers, he was able to become productive.

Gutenberg never forgave his betrayer. And he died a wretched, bitter old man without a dime to his name.

So who do you need to forgive?

It's time to get over it.

## Moving On

If Joseph hadn't dealt with his bitterness toward his brothers, how then would he have been able to deal with the bitterness that would soon come when he would be falsely accused by Potiphar's wife?

Joseph was on his way up the ladder to a remarkable position and responsibility. But God would not trust such a critical position to a vindictive and poisoned man, seething with resentment and dreams of revenge. So Joseph had to deal with the great evil that his brothers had done to him while it was still fresh. And deal with it he did. He knew that the Lord was in absolute control of his past, his present, and his future.

And that takes us right back to the fact that God is in control of every assignment of my life. Every assignment is part of the plan. That doesn't mean that every assignment will be exciting or fulfilling. But it does mean that every assignment is *preparation* for the ultimate work that God has for my life.

So as a result, no assignment is unimportant. Every assignment from the Lord has significance even though it may be humiliating and not what we would have chosen.

That's where Joseph was when he was sold into slavery. It was a humiliating, distasteful assignment. And Joseph had no possible way of knowing how important and strategic it was in preparing him for the ultimate work that God had ordained for him to do. Corrie wanted to help others learn to forgive those who had abused them and wronged them. So it was necessary, that, in the hidden places of her heart, she, too, would learn that lesson.

The same was true of Joseph. The hidden and hard work of forgiveness had to take place in his heart so that he could overcome the bitterness and hostility that threatened to undo him. That was the secret success that took place down deep. This is how Joseph moved from being a victim to a victor.

He got a grip on the providence of God.

He understood that every assignment was from the Lord. And that included slavery. He bowed the knee and submitted to the will of God. That is the definition of true success.

## Sometimes God Refuses Your Desired Assignment

Sometimes the Lord will stun you by not giving you an assignment that you really want. What a shattering disappointment that can be! You may be turned down by the college of your choice or left at the altar by someone you deeply wanted to marry. Or you may be a soldier who wants desperately to get into combat, but your superiors keep you in the States.

That's what happened to Dwight Eisenhower in World War I. He graduated from West Point, looking forward to an outstanding career in the military. And then in April 1917, America jumped into World War I. Eisenhower was elated that he would finally get a chance to lead troops in combat. But he was assigned to train the 57th Infantry in San Antonio. He desperately wanted to get into battle, but his hands were tied. So he threw all his energy into making those young recruits into exceptional soldiers. He didn't mope around in self-pity. He gave it his best shot. And as a result, once again his organizational skills in training were so outstanding that he was given a new command. He was to command and build the new Tanks Corps. It was an honor to be given the assignment. Maybe … but it also kept Eisenhower from where he really wanted to be—in the middle of the battle.

Finally the orders came to leave for France on November 18, 1918. But on November 11, World War I ended. He never made it into battle. "Eisenhower was deflated and depressed. He could hardly believe it had happened to him—he was a professional soldier who had missed action in the greatest war in history."[8] He thought the chance of a lifetime was gone. He would never have the opportunity to go into war again.

But what he didn't know was that some twenty years later, he would not only go into war, he would be in command of the war.

Eisenhower may have been deeply disappointed, but he didn't let himself get bitter toward his superiors who had kept him out of combat. He didn't rage, and he didn't complain. He kept doing his job to the best of his ability. And because of his discipline and attitude, those same superiors saw greatness in him. They kept him in mind and they didn't forget. That's why he was in command of the war he thought he would never see.

Every assignment is providential. For that matter, so is every assignment that you want but don't get. God is in control. He has a plan. And the more we know of God's providence, the more we can see His hand in the assignments that we want but don't get.

John Calvin was right in his observation: "When the light of divine providence has once shone upon a godly man, he is then relieved and set free not only from the extreme anxiety and fear that were pressing him before, but from every care."

So get over it.

He is in control of your life.

And He knows precisely what He is doing.

Chapter Five

# Sacked by God for a Ten-Yard Loss

## He Is in Control ...
## Over Grievous Setbacks

*"God often prospers us by impoverishing us."*
*—Thomas Watson*

There's an old story that has become part of the Federal Express corporate culture. Fred Smith, the visionary founder of the company, was always known as a great risk-taker. He had been flying planes since he was in high school and always enjoyed the thrill of being airborne.

On one occasion, however, Fred was feeling just a little bit bored. He was on a short, routine flight from Memphis to Little Rock, and when he reached the halfway point, he decided to have a little fun.

He flew the rest of the trip upside down.[1]

Sometimes we find ourselves flying through life upside down. But when that happens it's usually not our choice. Nothing can turn your life upside down and disorient you quicker that a grievous setback.

That's certainly what happened to Joseph.

And he wasn't the first or the last man to have his stomach turned upside down by the kick-in-the-gut sensation of a grievous—and totally unlooked-for—setback.

Martin Luther, the great reformer who stood for biblical truth against the whole world, often battled depression. He did his best to fight it off, but sometimes it would get the best of him.

On one occasion, he was losing the battle. Circumstances were piling up against him and he had just experienced another dismaying setback in his battle for truth. As a result, he holed up in his study for several days. Withdrawn and moody, he would come out for meals and then quickly return to his books. And everyone in the family knew what was going on.

After this had gone on for several days, his wife, Katie, walked into his study. She was dressed in black from head to toe. Luther looked at her and said, "Are you going to a funeral?"

"No," Katie replied. "Since you are acting like God is dead, I thought I would come in and mourn with you."[2]

God isn't dead, but He sometimes acts strangely.

He allows us to experience grievous setbacks. And when He does, it baffles us, confuses us, and makes us wonder, *Where is the goodness of God?*

In an earlier chapter we discussed cross providences—the dilemmas we experience when God's dealings with us don't add up. In a cross providence, you begin to feel God is working against you, rather than for you. When we get hit with a grievous setback, it's always a cross providence. And they make absolutely no sense to us. When they hit us, as with Martin Luther, we can quickly find ourselves duped into depression, because it looks like God is dead.

## The Interstates of Providence

I'm sure that you have encountered a grievous setback. I know that I have. And before it's all over on this earth, we'll probably endure a few more. When those setbacks blindside us, we are shocked, then stunned, and then confused as to what to do next. Our well-laid plans have been turned upside down. Suddenly we have no clue what we're doing or where we're going.

It's in times like those that you need the map of the Word of God. And the more you know the Word of God, the more quickly you will come to grips with those sudden devastating circumstances that crash into your life. The more you know the interstate highways of providential actions in the lives of God's people, the more you will understand that He uses setbacks, troubles, and tragedies to bring good to His people and glory to His name. He controls and utilizes grievous setbacks to bring about His purpose for your life.

It was Matthew Henry who stated that "God sometimes raises difficulties in the lives of His people that He may have the glory of subduing them, and helping His people over them." You only learn that truth from the Scriptures. You see that principle time and time again in both testaments.

When you are making your way through uncharted territory, it's a very good idea to have a map. It's an even better idea to know how to read the map. But the best scenario of all in new territory is to have the guide who actually drew up the map leading you.

Joseph had to have been shocked by his success. As he was on his way to Egypt to be sold into a life of slavery, the last thing he could have imagined was that God was going to give him great success. In the last chapter, we saw the remarkable providence in his life that led him to overseeing the great estate of Potiphar. But that certainly wasn't what he was expecting when they put him on the auction block.

With all of that success came the perks. Slaves don't usually get privileges, but Joseph was no average slave. He was a successful man, and he probably couldn't believe how well his life had turned out. He had a challenging job, an employer who trusted him completely, and privileges and rewards beyond what any slave could ever expect. That's why he had that Platinum Egyptian Express card. Most slaves didn't have the credit rating to get one of those babies.

Now obviously we don't know what perks Joseph had—but we can use our imaginations. Because of Joseph's obvious gifting and success, he had been promoted and given privileges. He oversaw *everything* for Potiphar. That's power. And where there's power, privilege and status always follow right behind. That's why he was the only slave who had a membership at the country club. And he was the only slave who ever tipped the caddies out of his own pocket.

Here's the thing about success. When we achieve it, we never want to lose it. We want to keep the increased pay, the elevated authority, and the significant boost in privileges. Joseph was no different. Do you think he wanted to lose any of that? Of course he didn't. When any of us experience a degree of success, we want to see that it keeps on going.

But God had more important things in mind for Joseph than his own personal comfort. What God had in mind for Joseph would have taken his breath away. One day Joseph would rule over *all* the palaces and estates of Egypt, including Potiphar's, and including Pharaoh's. Joseph would be like a father to Pharaoh (Gen. 45:8), and therefore the most powerful and influential man on the face of the earth.

But before all of that could happen, Joseph had to be prepared. His character had to be tested and refined. So he was about to go through a grievous setback that he never saw coming.

Because of this great plan of God of which Joseph knew nothing, he was about to lose his power, his privileges, and his success—and he would lose it all in a matter of minutes. And further, *it would be through no fault or poor decision of his own.* He would lose his position and prominence because he chose to obey God and refuse sexual sin.

In the short term, it would cost him dearly. It would prove to be not just a setback, but a grievous setback. And when he was thrown into the jail for doing what was right, it was also a cross providence.

At the moment, however, it made absolutely no sense. How could this be good, and how could God ever turn this into good? He simply couldn't see or imagine it.

But God's ways are beyond our comprehension, and He had so much more in mind for Joseph that he could have ever imagined. Those were the hidden reasons behind what was about to happen to Joseph. Once again, God was in control of every event that was occurring in Joseph's life. He had experienced success and it was good. But he was about to have his world shattered by a grievous setback. And God was behind the scenes, orchestrating the entire episode, rewarding the good decision with bad consequences. That is a classic example of a cross providence.

Cross providences, so rarely taught in today's church, are embedded in Scripture from the front cover to the back. Because we have been so deprived when it comes to this aspect of providence, it would be worthwhile to take a closer look. And here's the good news about cross providences: They are remarkably encouraging. If you're in the middle of a cross providence that has caused you to experience a grievous setback, you can actually bank on the fact that God will one day turn it for your benefit. That's flat-out what He loves to do.

## This Is a Test

Joseph was grateful to God for his success and his promotion. But God had an even greater promotion in mind for Joseph. I'm sure Joseph would have been happy just to keep things going the way that they were. But God's ways are not our ways. We would like our successes to keep rolling along according to our own goals and objectives. But God is free to interrupt our plans at any time in order to achieve His superior plan in our lives. God has no problem in taking success away when it serves His purposes. So here's a principle to keep in mind:

*Before God promotes, God tests.*

If there is any doubt about that principle, Psalm 105:16–19 proves it from the life of Joseph:

> And He called for a famine upon the land;
> He broke the whole staff of bread.

He sent a man before them,
Joseph, who was sold as a slave.
They afflicted his feet with fetters,
He himself was laid in irons;
Until the time that his word came to pass,
The word of the LORD tested him.

God had a good reason for Joseph's grievous setback, but this godly young man just couldn't see it yet. He was about to undergo another excruciating test.

To enter college it is necessary to take the SAT (Scholastic Aptitude Test). In order to be promoted by God, it is also necessary to pass the SAT. In God's vocabulary, the SAT stands for Setback And Trial. And in Joseph's case it would also stand for Sex And Temptation. A rich Egyptian chick who was botoxed, nipped, tucked, and siliconed had him in her sights.

Now Joseph was handsome in form and appearance. And after a time his master's wife cast her eyes on Joseph and said, "Lie with me." But he refused and said to his master's wife, "Behold, because of me my master has no concern about anything in the house, and he has put everything that he has in my charge. He is not greater in this house than I am, nor has he kept back anything from me except yourself, because you are his wife. How then can I do this great wickedness and sin against God?" And as she spoke to Joseph day after day, he would not listen to her, to lie beside her or to be with her. But one day, when he went into the house to do his work and none of the men of the house was there in the house, she caught him by his garment, saying, "Lie with me." But he left his garment in her hand and fled and got out of the house. And as soon as she saw that he had left his garment in her hand

and had fled out of the house, she called to the men of her household and said to them, "See, he has brought among us a Hebrew to laugh at us. He came in to me to lie with me, and I cried out with a loud voice. And as soon as he heard that I lifted up my voice and cried out, he left his garment beside me and fled and got out of the house." Then she laid up his garment by her until his master came home, and she told him the same story, saying, "The Hebrew servant, whom you have brought among us, came in to me to laugh at me. But as soon as I lifted up my voice and cried, he left his garment beside me and fled out of the house." (Gen. 39:6–18 ESV)

There are tests and there are tests … and for a healthy young man in his twenties, this was a tough one. Joseph was about to be tested in the area of sexual purity. He was young, good looking, in great shape, and at his sexual peak. He probably worked out six days a week—three days cardio and three days on weights. This young Hebrew was a steroid-free stud.

As we have noted, Joseph's life was in the ascendancy, and everybody could see it.

And then along came the trophy wife.

We really don't know much about her, but we can surmise at least this much: She was a wealthy, spoiled, and pampered pagan woman, utterly devoid of any morals whatsoever. And when she spotted young, fit Joseph, she decided that she wanted to sleep with him.

Life had been good for Joseph. He was enjoying all of the fruits of success. He thought his worst days were behind him. But then this woman showed up. Not just any woman, but his master's wife! We don't know her name, but I like to call her Predator. And she was going to make Joseph's life miserable.

So why was Joseph in this set of circumstances? How did Joseph get in such a difficult situation? God intended to test the resolve of Joseph's obedience by bringing him in contact with this loose woman.

And she didn't take no for an answer.

She kept coming back to Joseph, day after day, hoping to entice him to break his integrity before God and her own husband.

That's why 1 Timothy 4:16 (NIV) says, "watch your life and doctrine closely." How we live our lives and what we believe about God and His Word must be watched very closely.

I bring this up for a reason. What Joseph believed about God determined how Joseph responded to sexual temptation. His behavior was not separated from his belief. His behavior was tied to his belief and the result of his belief.

Joseph knew that God is sovereign. But he also believed that he was responsible to God for his choices. Joseph watched closely over his life and his doctrine—they were more important to him than his success.

Yes, Joseph knew that God is in control. He fully realized that God was in charge of his life. But he also knew that he was responsible to walk carefully and prudently on the path where God had placed him. Here is the biblical balance we must always keep before us: God is sovereign—but we are responsible.

Joseph had struck the balance. When this wealthy, pagan Egyptian woman hit on Joseph, he was ready with his response. Joseph had to make a decision about this woman. Would he sleep with her or not? And he had to make that decision every day because she was hitting on him every day. This wasn't a one-time test. It was daily—she never left him alone. It doesn't take much imagination to realize that she used every feminine wile in the book to get him to succumb.

The emphasis in this book has been on the fact that God is sovereign and that all things are under His providential care and plan. *He is in control!*

That's the message. But that central fact of our existence does not negate the fact that man is responsible for his choices and decisions!

This is all tied up in Joseph's sterling response to the woman's godless invitation: *"How then could I do this great evil and sin against God?"*

Joseph neither hesitated nor rationalized. He didn't minimize or downplay the seriousness of the temptation—and that's why he ran, not walked, out of that cloud of perfume and out of that room! He called her invitation a *"great evil."* It was absolutely clear in his mind. He could not and would not betray his sovereign God.

But Joseph was human, 100 percent male, and it couldn't have been easy. God moved Predator directly into Joseph's path to test the young man's heart and will. As the shameless woman plied her wares day after day, God was testing Joseph's character, purity, and reliability.

One day, Predator thought she had set the perfect trap. There was no one else in the house, and when Joseph came into her sights, she grabbed him, pulling him toward her bed. But instead of falling for her sexual proposal, he literally ran out of the room.

That was the final straw for Predator. You've heard the old saying, haven't you? "Hell hath no fury like a woman scorned." Well, as far as she was concerned, she had been scorned by Joseph's countless refusals. And she decided to get even.

> As soon as his master heard the words that his wife spoke to him, "This is the way your servant treated me," his anger was kindled. And Joseph's master took him and put him into the prison, the place where the king's prisoners were confined, and he was there in prison. (Gen. 39:19–20 ESV)

## No Parole for Purity

The next thing Joseph knew, he was being cuffed and escorted off to the dungeon. Why was Joseph in jail? What had he done wrong? *Nothing.* He had done what was right! And now he was paying for it because a wicked woman had lied. She had perjured herself in order to ruin Joseph's life. If she couldn't steal his purity, then she would make sure that he paid the penalty.

It was the London preacher of the 1600s Thomas Watson who said, "a perjurer is the devil's excrement."

That's precisely what this woman was. Because of her lying and vindictive charges, Joseph's career as a successful household CEO was at an end. And now he was in jail.

For Joseph, this was a grievous setback. It was a cross providence. He had done what was right and now he was to suffer the consequences. Everything he had worked so hard for was gone. His position, his privileges, and his power in Potiphar's estate dissolved like a puff of smoke. This wasn't just any setback. This was a grievous setback.

*But God is in control of grievous setbacks.*

*And God often works strangely.*

Furthermore, there was a reason for the setback. In fact, it was a brilliant, heaven-conceived strategy. But at that moment, sitting on the damp floor of some dark and smelly dungeon, Joseph couldn't see it.

> But the Lord was with Joseph and showed him steadfast love and gave him favor in the sight of the keeper of the prison. And the keeper of the prison put Joseph in charge of all the prisoners who were in the prison. Whatever was done there, he was the one who did it. The keeper of the prison paid no attention to anything that was in Joseph's charge, because the Lord was with him. And whatever he did, the Lord made it succeed. (Gen. 39:21–23 ESV)

There's that life-changing phrase again! *"The Lord was with Joseph."* We first saw that phrase back when Jacob's kidnapped son was purchased by Potiphar, and now, here it is again.

Have you experienced a grievous setback? It may not seem like it, but the Lord is with you. Could it be that He's up to something you can't see?

## We Interrupt This Program ...

I want to interrupt this look at Joseph's battle with sexual temptation to make a point: The grievous setback can sometimes be professional instead of sexual. For that matter, it can be financial—or emotional or physical. But for Ravi Zacharias, at a key point in his life, it was a *professional* grievous setback.

Ravi Zacharias is an evangelist and apologist who has been used by the Lord all over the world. But as a young man he felt confused about the path of his life. And then one day, he was sure that he had found it. He decided to become an air-force pilot in his home country of India. Along with a friend, Ravi traveled to a distant base where he was to take the grueling tests required for entrance into the pilot program. Several hundred young men were competing for just a handful of slots. In his book *Walking from East to West*, Ravi explains:

> After a full battery of mental, physical, and endurance tests, I was overjoyed to learn that, out of the few hundred competing, I had placed third and my buddy fourth. The officers in charge seemed impressed, knowing I had good physical endurance because of all the sports I played.
>
> That night I called home excitedly. "I'm going to make it. All that's left is the interview with the senior officer tomorrow."
>
> For the first time, I could tell by my dad's tone that he was proud. I was told there would be a big celebration party for me when I arrived home.
>
> The next morning, I sat confidently in front of the senior officer—a gruff, heavyset man—ready for anything. After many questions about my values and my hopes and dreams, he startled me with a direct statement.
>
> "Son, I'm rejecting you," he said abruptly.

"Huh?" I thought, dumbstruck.

"You're being turned down by the air force," he repeated.

I was stunned into silence. I had a hard time believing this. Before I could ask why, he explained. "This job is about killing, and psychologically you are unfit to kill."

What could I say to that? It hit me hard. He must have seen the tears welling up in my eyes, because he said, "I'm doing you a favor, young man. Believe it."

When I stepped off the train in Delhi, a crowd of family and friends was waiting for me with garlands. Talk about a low point—it was absolutely humiliating! I struggled with it; but deep inside, my concern was for a reason other than another failure. I wondered, "Is this God stopping my steps?"

I pondered much on this for the next few days. Finally someone suggested that I go and talk to a visiting missionary who was staying at the YWCA, a man named Russell Self from Canada. I gathered myself to go and see him, and I ended up pouring out my heart to him over my disappointment.

Mr. Self sat listening and nodding his head, and I thought, "He must be thinking, 'This kid is just taking up my time.'" Instead, he responded with sage counsel.

"We can be so sure of ourselves at times, " he said, "that we don't know there are some doors that we shouldn't be entering. God not only opens doors; he shuts them too. Sometimes very painfully."

"This has to be one of those times," I thought. But knowing that didn't lessen my pain.

"What we often miss," Mr. Self added, "is that some of those shut doors reveal the most important clues as to where God wants us to go."

What was the clue for me here?

"Remember this from Psalm 37," he said. "'The steps of a good man are ordered by the Lord, and he delighteth in his way.' God has it all in order, Ravi. I believe that's what you're going to know from this." Then he opened his Bible, leaned forward, and read: "Commit thy way unto the Lord; trust also in him; and he shall bring it to pass."[3]

Ravi wanted to be in the cockpit. The Lord wanted him to speak and write to millions. When he was a young man, he had no clue that was the plan. All he knew was that he had suffered a grievous setback.

## Puzzled in Prison

The Lord was with Joseph in Potiphar's house and now the Lord was with him in prison. And watch this! The Lord began to prosper him and give him favor with the chief jailer. Before he knew it, Joseph was running the whole prison. Here we go again!

Joseph loved the success that he experienced in Potiphar's palace. He had learned all kinds of lessons as Potiphar gave him more and more responsibility. He discovered gifts he didn't know that he had. This was a huge house, so he had to learn budgeting, forecasting, inventory, and human resources. But after awhile, he had learned everything he could learn in that position. He didn't know it, but he had milked that situation for all the lessons he could get.

He liked his position and his perks. But he couldn't stay there, because God had more for him to learn. Where would he learn those lessons? He would learn them in Pharaoh's jail. And in a very short amount of time, Joseph was running the jail as he had governed Potiphar's great estate.

It was another step in his preparation.

That's what grievous setbacks really are: God interrupts our plans, hopes, and dreams in order to accomplish His plan in our lives.

Sometimes when we're blindsided by a severe trial, it staggers us. If we're not careful, the shock and disorientation of such a serious loss has the potential to send us into a downward spiral toward depression and even despair.

One of Winston Churchill's closest friends was an eccentric and brilliant physicist, Professor F. A. Lindemann. The professor was an utterly unconventional genius. And nothing proved his peculiar approach to life more than something that he accomplished during World War I.

> In 1916 RAF pilots were dying daily in nosedives. At the Royal Aircraft Establishment in Farnborough, Lindemann had worked out, with mathematical precision, a maneuver which, he said, would bring any aircraft out of a tailspin. The pilots said it wouldn't work. The Prof taught himself to fly, took off without a parachute, deliberately sent the aircraft into a spin, and brought it out so successfully that mastering his solution became required of every beginning flyer.[4]

When an unexpected hardship slams into our lives, so does the potential for a devastating spin into depression. We would all like to think we could pull out of that nosedive, but sometimes it's almost more than we can manage. The solution, however, doesn't lie in a mathematical formula but in a biblical formula.

## Pulling Out of the Spin

Psalm 119:68 states the life-changing truth: *"You [God] are good and do good."*

When we are blindsided by a shocking and sudden reversal in our comfortable circumstances, we immediately lose our balance and equilibrium. We begin to spin downward out of control into depression. In those moments we must reach for the ripcord—the ripcord that produces truth in the midst of chaos.

When life as you know it and as you like it falls apart, what do you reach for? You must reach for the truth. You may be hurt, you may be speechless, you may be unjustly accused. What is your anchor in times of great distress and loss? It is the truth of the goodness of God. The Lord is good and does good.

Our first reaction when we suffer loss is to question the goodness of God. I have done that and so have you. But may I be frank here? We must learn to grow up in our faith. We must get hold of our hurt and our disappointment and anchor our lives and our emotions on the truth of God. And the truth is simply this: God is good, does good, and is in control of all things.

I may not see it, I may not feel it, I may not understand it, and I may not appreciate it. But this one thing I know: God is good. And if He who controls all things has permitted this grievous setback to come into my life, then He will show me His goodness in some way that I cannot possibly see at the present moment.

## When God Kidnaps

I go back to Martin Luther. Actually, before we go back to Luther, let's go back to Johannes Gutenberg, the brilliant inventor of the printing press who died in bitterness. Let me show you how God used a grievous setback in Luther's life to intersect with Gutenberg's invention. This is so far out of left field that only God could have thought this one up.

When Luther, a Roman Catholic priest, stood up to the Roman Catholic Church in 1517 for their radical departure from the teachings of the Bible, he became a marked man. His life was in serious danger. As he made his way to Worms, Germany, to defend himself before the emperor, he fully expected to be burned at the stake. This was the common punishment for those who stood against the authority of the church.

Luther refused to change his position before the emperor. He was given a day to reconsider. When he appeared again before the emperor, he was directly asked if he would recant the teachings in his books. His reply is now classic:

> Unless I am convinced by the testimony of the Scriptures or by clear reason (for I do not trust either in the pope or in councils alone, since it is well known that they have often erred and contradicted themselves), I am bound by the Scriptures I have quoted and my conscience is captive to the Word of God. I cannot and will not retract anything, since it is neither safe nor right to go against conscience. I cannot do otherwise, here I stand, may God help me, amen.[5]

Immediate chaos broke out. Luther was escorted out of the building, but there were shouts that he should be thrown into the fire. And Luther was overheard saying to himself, "I am finished."[6]

Although promised safe passage back home to Wittenberg, Luther was required to return in three weeks. As he was making his way home in his wagon with his friends, his group was suddenly attacked by armed men. Luther didn't know if they were the emperor's soldiers or the pope's, but he knew that they meant him harm. Before he was kidnapped, he managed to grab his Greek New Testament and his Hebrew Bible. He then rode off with his captors to an unknown fate. Without question, he could only imagine the very worst.

It was a grievous setback. He thought he had at least three weeks to get his life in order. But now the end seemed near. It was a bitter disappointment and cross providence. Why in the world would God allow him to be kidnapped at the worst possible time?

But later that night when they arrived at a remote castle, he discovered his captors had been sent by his good friend Frederick of Wise, elector of Saxony. He thought the kidnapping would mean the end of his life. It turned out he had been kidnapped by his friends in order to *save* his life.

At the castle, he exchanged his monk's robe for the clothes of a knight. He was known as Knight George.

Luther was grateful he had been spared, but became very lonely at the castle. He was away from his friends and his students. He resisted staying at the castle for months upon end, but it was the only smart thing to do.

And then he got an idea. Why not use the time that he had been given to translate the Bible into German? If the people could actually read the Bible for themselves, it would make all the difference! Up until now, only priests could read the Bible since it was in Latin. But if he could put it into the everyday language of the people, it would unleash the Word of God in their hearts.

That's precisely what Luther did. The Bible that he translated into German rocked all of Europe. And it is still the standard German Bible today.[7]

Luther's time in Wartburg Castle changed the lives of millions who have read his translation of Scripture over the centuries. He thought he was going to die by fire—but God intended him to set all of Europe on fire by the power of His Word. That is the beauty of the cross providences of God.

And there's one more nugget to the story. Gutenberg's printing presses, which were now set up across Germany, began turning out Luther's Bible by the thousands upon thousands. It was one thing for Luther to have translated the Bible—it was another for it to be printed in mass quantities and distributed to the people.

One hundred years before, it couldn't have happened. But the providence of God was at work in the lives of both Gutenberg and Luther. And the Word of God went forth and brought about a Reformation.

When we get hit with a providence that is cross-eyed and makes no sense to us, we need to take a step back, let our racing pulse slow down for a moment, and remind ourselves that God is working (somehow) on our behalf.

When Luther was kidnapped, all he could see was a grievous setback. He had absolutely no clue that God would turn it into an amazing advancement of the gospel.

## The Way It Wasn't

Joseph must have been in a state of shock that first night in the Egyptian dungeon. Everything that had been given to him had been taken away. As far as he knew, he would never have another opportunity again. He could see no hope for the future. His reputation had been nuked by a very powerful and well-connected woman. From Joseph's perspective, his future in Egypt was nil.

Now … imagine the Lord feeling sorry for this young man in his hurt and disappointment. Imagine Him standing by Joseph at midnight in the dungeon, and whispering …

*"Joseph, listen to Me. I know you are hurting and I know that you don't understand why this has happened. I know this is devastating for you. So I'm about to do something I don't normally do. I'm going to go ahead and tell you why I put you in here. Ready? Here's the scoop.*

*"Before long, you're going to be running this jail. I will give you favor with the chief jailer, and he will turn everything over to you just as Potiphar did. You're about to learn things in this place you couldn't learn in Potiphar's household. That's why I put you in here. Before long, two men who work for Pharaoh will be thrown into prison. They will have dreams and you will interpret their dreams. One will live and one will die, just as you say. When the one man goes back to work for Pharaoh, you will ask him not to forget you, but he will forget. I will make him forget you. You'll be in here for two more years.*

*"Are you tracking with Me, Joseph? At the end of that time, I'll make Pharaoh have a dream that will scare him to death. He will call his advisers together, but none of them will be able to give meaning to his dream. Then I will make the cupbearer remember you. He will tell Pharaoh about you and the dream you interpreted. Pharaoh will then summon you, and you will stand before him and tell him that I am giving seven years of prosperity and then seven years of famine. You will then instruct him to appoint a man to administrate the prosperity so the world can survive the famine. He will appoint you to the task and make you the second most powerful man in the world.*

*"After that, Joseph, I will then bring your father and your brothers to Egypt, and you'll be reunited with them. You and your brothers will be the twelve tribes of Israel, and through your family I will bring My Son into the world. He will be born of a virgin and will give His life a ransom for many. That's why you're in here. Got it?"*

And Joseph answers, "No kidding? That's unreal. How long did You say I have to be in here?"

*"Two years."*

"And You'll take care of me and give me everything I need in this place?"

*"I will."*

"Okay. I'm good with that."

But that's not what happened. In fact, Joseph really didn't have a clue.

We don't walk by sight; we walk by faith. When we suffer a grievous setback, God doesn't lay out in detail why it has occurred and what He plans to do to fix it.

He asks us to trust Him, believing that He is good and that He will do good—even though we can't see evidence of it at the time.

That's the purpose of the grievous setback.

And that's why you won't be in it much longer.

## Chapter Six

# When Hope Gets Intercepted

## He Is in Control ...
## Over Broken Hopes

*"Hope is the pillar that holds up the world."*
—*Pliny the Elder*

Howard Head was a lousy athlete who radically changed two sports: skiing and tennis. And it was all because of his broken hope to be a capable athlete.

Howard had wanted to be a good skier since he was a kid. But because of his poor athletic ability, just about every time he tried to tackle a slope, he wound up breaking his wood skis. Even so, he held on to the hope of one day becoming a skillful skier. That hope may have looked pretty faint to Howard at times, but not faint enough to keep him from trying something that seemed crazy at the time.

The more Howard thought about it, the more he convinced himself that his problem with skiing wasn't his skills on the slopes, it was the skis! So in 1941 Howard Head, who was a brilliant engineer, took $6,000 in poker winnings, and focused his entire life on building skis out of aircraft materials.[1] His friends thought he was nuts. Everyone knew the best skis were made out of hickory. Undaunted, Howard invested several years developing a composite ski that was virtually unbreakable—and the skiing world was changed forever. Head Skis became the dominant company in the industry.

Eventually, Howard Head sold his company and became a multimillionaire. Along the way, he also realized his dream of becoming a better skier.

Now rich and retired, Howard built a tennis court in his backyard and spent $5,000 on tennis lessons. But once again, his lack of athletic ability seemed to stymie him. He bought a ball machine to help him practice on his own, but he became convinced that the Prince ball machine could be improved. So he bought the company and spent months improving the machine. Within a very short time, his improved ball machine captured 50 percent of the market.[2]

But he was still a lousy tennis player.

Then it dawned on him that his trouble might be with the racquet. He should make it bigger. Once again, his friends thought he was nuts—it was against the rules to have a bigger racquet. Howard Head looked up the rules and discovered that there were no regulations on the size of the racquet. As far as the rules were concerned, you could play tennis with a waffle iron. So he began to work on an oversized racquet that was two inches wider and three inches longer. He personally played with it, amazing even himself at the improvement in his game.

After much trial and error and extensive tests in the lab, Howard eventually had test results that proved the sweet spot of his racquet was 20 percent greater than a normal racquet. The Prince racquet became the gold standard in tennis, and in 1982 Howard Head sold Prince Tennis for $62 million. Because he had virtually no hope of becoming a better tennis player unless he improved the equipment, Howard Head did just that. And everyone benefited.

When most people lose hope, however, it's usually about things significantly more important—and nearer to the heart—than skiing or tennis.

How important is hope? It's a fact of life that a man can live without water for only several days, and without food for a matter of weeks.

But nothing kills the heart of a man more than the absence of hope.

When hope is gone, life is gone.

## Playing the Game of Life

Joseph wasn't worried about tennis. He was concerned about the course of his life. Although he was only two years away from a great achievement, this young man had something else to accomplish first. He had to fight off broken hopes.

Solomon, in his God-given wisdom, gave the ultimate diagnosis when hopes are broken: "Hope deferred makes the heart sick" (Prov. 13:12).

That pretty much sums it up.

When we get our hopes up and it looks like they are just about to be fulfilled—and then they're not—well, it makes us sick at heart. There is no ache deeper than heartache. And we all have experienced it.

Broken hopes are a kick in the gut.

When big hopes get broken, it can be hell on earth.

Broken hopes often go hand in hand with disappointment and sorrow. We experience hopelessness when we are crushed and beaten up by the disappointments and sorrows of life. You've been there and so have I.

> *I walked a mile with pleasure,*
> *She chatted all the way,*
> *But left me none the wiser*
> *For all she had to say.*
>
> *I walked a mile with sorrow*
> *And ne'er a word said she,*

*But oh the things I learned from her,*
*When sorrow walked with me.*

Garth Brooks isn't known for his theological writings, but a number of years ago he came up with a song that contained a lot of theology. The title is simply "Some of God's Greatest Gifts Are Unanswered Prayers."

We see a job we want or a person we want to marry or a dream for our life, and we begin to pray. And sometimes, God says no. Unanswered prayers often result in broken hopes. That country song tells the story of a man who goes to his high school reunion accompanied by his wife. And there he meets his high school sweetheart, the girl he so desperately wanted to marry. That prayer wasn't answered, and it broke his heart at the time. But now he is holding the hand of the woman who was the answer to the prayer. Some of God's greatest gifts are unanswered prayers. But sometimes, as we have seen, you don't see it until years down the road. And then you have to look backward.

God is in control of unanswered prayers, and He is in control when our hopes get broken. The providence of God is overseeing your life and bringing about what is best for you. At this very moment, He is weaving your life together for His glory and honor. And He knows precisely what He is doing, even when our hopes are broken.

Broken hopes are one of the tools in God's workshop.

"[Just] as there are tools of all sorts and sizes in the shop of Providence, so there is a most skillful hand that uses them, and [is it not true] that they could no more produce such effects of themselves than the axe, saw, or chisel can cut or carve a rough log into a beautiful figure without the hand of the skillful craftsman?"[3]

Who but God could use shattered hopes as a providential tool to bring about His best in our lives? He is truly the skillful Craftsman.

This is displayed very prominently in the story of Joseph.

We last left Joseph in prison. As you recall, he was not there because he had done something wrong. He was there because he had followed the Lord. And as a result, he had been falsely accused.

But through the goodness and favor of God, Joseph was soon placed in charge of the whole prison. It was God's good pleasure to have him quickly catch the eye of the chief jailer, and the next thing we read is that Joseph had been given the responsibility of a very large and important institution.

As gracious as God was to give him the responsibility of running the prison, it's not an assignment Joseph would have treasured. He didn't want to be there in the first place. Would you? Of course not.

Now two things are going to happen in the next chapter of Joseph's life.

*His hopes will be raised. His hopes will be broken.* That sounds like a chapter to avoid at all cost.

But it's all part of the plan.

## The Wine Man and the Baker

Some time after this, the cupbearer of the king of Egypt and his baker committed an offense against their lord the king of Egypt. And Pharaoh was angry with his two officers, the chief cupbearer and the chief baker, and he put them in custody in the house of the captain of the guard, in the prison where Joseph was confined. The captain of the guard appointed Joseph to be with them, and he attended them. They continued for some time in custody.

And one night they both dreamed—the cupbearer and the baker of the king of Egypt, who were confined in the prison—each his own dream, and each dream with its own interpretation. When Joseph came to them in the morning, he saw that they were troubled. So he asked Pharaoh's officers who were with him in custody in his master's house, "Why are your faces downcast today?" They said to him, "We have had dreams, and there is no one to interpret them." And Joseph said to them, "Do not interpretations belong to God? Please tell them to me."

So the chief cupbearer told his dream to Joseph and said to him, "In my dream there was a vine before me, and on the vine there were three branches. As soon as it budded, its blossoms shot forth, and the clusters ripened into grapes. Pharaoh's cup was in my hand, and I took the grapes and pressed them into Pharaoh's cup and placed the cup in Pharaoh's hand." Then Joseph said to him, "This is its interpretation: the three branches are three days. In three days Pharaoh will lift up your head and restore you to your office, and you shall place Pharaoh's cup in his hand as formerly, when you were his cupbearer. Only remember me, when it is well with you, and please do me the kindness to mention me to Pharaoh, and so get me out of this house. For I was indeed stolen out of the land of the Hebrews, and here also I have done nothing that they should put me into the pit." (Gen. 40:1–15 ESV)

So let's put ourselves in Joseph's sandals for a minute here. He's in prison, falsely accused of being a sexual predator. He's desperate to get out of that place, but now he's been elevated to executive associate warden. He's got a corner office, someone brings him a latte when he shows up in the morning, and he has an administrative assistant to help him oversee this vast operation.

And then one day, these two men who work for Pharaoh are thrown into the jail. They had both done something to really tick Pharaoh off. Now, these two men weren't insignificant. On the contrary, they were very strategic in Pharaoh's administration. Every head of state will often put on lavish state dinners for visiting dignitaries—sometimes four or five times a week. That's where the baker would come in. This guy wasn't making doughnuts down at Krispy Kreme. He was a world-class chef who was responsible to put out the very best of cuisine for the guests of Pharaoh. If he were around today, he'd have his own show on the Food Channel.

Even more important was the cupbearer—the trusted man who tasted the wine before it was offered to Pharaoh. When the cupbearer would take a sip of the wine, everyone would hold their breath for a minute, waiting to see if he would keel over and die. If he didn't keel over, the wine was safe and the paramedics could go back to watching the ball game. The cupbearer protected Pharaoh from being poisoned by offering up his own life, if necessary, at every meal. He was a trusted and valued member of Pharaoh's inner circle.

So one day these two officials showed up in the prison Joseph was running. Joseph became acquainted with these two men and, as time went by, developed some degree of relationship with them. The men had been in this prison under Joseph's charge for some time, when something very unusual occurred. On the same night, they both had dreams that significantly confused and depressed them. When Joseph noticed their demeanor the next morning, he said, in essence, "What's up?"

The gloomy officials responded that they had experienced unsettling dreams during the night.

Joseph asked them to describe the dreams. They couldn't figure out what the dreams meant, but as Joseph reminded them, God was able to make the interpretations clear.

As they related the dreams they had experienced, God instantly gave Joseph the interpretation, clear and to the point. The message to the cupbearer was that in three days he would be back on the job, performing his duties for Pharaoh as before. The message to the baker was that in three days he would be hanging from a rope.

On the third day, everything came about just as the Lord had said. And when the summons came from Pharaoh for the cupbearer to come back to work, here's what happened to Joseph: *His hopes were raised dramatically.* As Joseph served that indefinite sentence in the Egyptian slammer, he had to be wondering if he would ever get out. He couldn't call the ACLU, and he couldn't call an attorney. This wasn't America; it was Egypt. He was in that prison for the duration, perhaps for the rest of his life.

But now …?

Now he had an inside connection! The very man responsible for Pharaoh's life and welfare was now a friend. Joseph had done him a favor, providing him with encouragement in a tight spot, so maybe now the cupbearer would put in a good word for him. Surely he would!

This was the first ray of hope Joseph had experienced in who knows how long. Joseph must have felt like Howard Head when he got his new racquet.

It couldn't have just been an accident that these two guys ended up in prison with him. And it was certainly no accident that God had provided him with a spot-on interpretation! And great news at that. This was no accident, and it didn't happen by chance! God had worked this out, and this man would become Joseph's ticket out of prison. With one word to Pharaoh he could have Joseph released.

Wouldn't you be thinking something like that if you were in Joseph's place? Of course you would.

Now if you doubt that Joseph's hopes were raised, note again what he said to the cupbearer as he was being released: "Only remember me, when it is well with you, and please do me the kindness to mention me to Pharaoh, and so get me out of this house. For I was indeed stolen out of the land of the Hebrews, and here also I have done nothing that they should put me into the pit" (Gen. 40:14–15 ESV).

There it is! Mention me to Pharaoh and get me out of here! And notice that he mentions to the cupbearer that his hopes had already been broken twice. First, his hopes were smashed when his own brothers sold him down the river into slavery, and then, just when he was regaining a little of his equilibrium, he got slapped with a false rape charge.

So in essence, the last words that Joseph says to this guy on his way out are, *"Please don't forget me!"*

So what did the guy do?

He forgot him.

## The Silence of God

So what would happen now?

The answer is a big fat zero. Absolutely nothing would happen. And that was the broken hope.

Joseph kept waiting for the phone to ring, but it never did. He would check his voicemail five times a day—zippo. He kept checking his e-mail, thinking he would hear from the cupbearer—but nothing.

The silence was deafening.

Wasn't it C. S. Lewis who said that God speaks to us in our comfort but shouts to us in our pain? Joseph was in pain. His hopes had been deferred again, and once again he was heartsick. For the third time in his life, his hopes were broken, and this time it looked irreversible.

I'm reminded of a news account I read a few years back, when a large school of tuna was running off the coast of Cape Cod, Massachusetts—a very rare occurrence. A run of tuna hadn't been seen in New England for forty-seven years. Catching tuna, of course, can be very lucrative. Some Japanese buyers were laying out as much as $50,000 for a large bluefin tuna.

The word got out that the tuna were out there for the taking, just thirty miles off the coast. You didn't need a license or experience. Just a boat and the right equipment. A lot of guys heard what they could get for a tuna and thought it would be a good thing to do a little tuna fishing. They got in their small boats and headed out to sea. And many of them were very successful. But there's a difference between catching a tuna and landing a tuna.

On September 23, the *Christi Anne* capsized while doing battle with a tuna. On the same day, another small boat, *Basic Instinct*, met the same outcome. The boat's owner had fifty grand in his sights, but he ended up losing his boat and nearly losing his life. Another boat, *Official Business*, a nice twenty-eight footer, was swamped after it tried to land a 600-pound tuna on board. The tuna literally pulled the boat underwater.[4]

That's what you call a broken hope. You're "that" close to the biggest strike of your life ... but you can't land it.

When Joseph said his parting words to the cupbearer, that cupbearer was his $50,000 tuna. But when the cupbearer forgot him, Joseph's hopes sank faster than a small boat being pulled under by a 400-pound bluefin tuna. Joseph got his hopes up that the cupbearer could be his ticket out of jail. But then his hopes started to capsize when he never heard back from him.

Although Joseph couldn't have known it at the time, he was right on the money about the cupbearer and what that official of Pharaoh could do for him. He was also right that none of it had been by accident. It was a truly significant connection that the Lord gave to him.

But the cupbearer totally spaced. Back on the job again, he forgot all about the guy in prison who could interpret dreams. How could he forget something like that? There's only one explanation: The Lord made him forget. It simply wasn't time yet. Two years down the road he would suddenly remember Joseph. And he would remember because the Lord would make him remember.

Proverbs 21:1 (ESV) explains, "The king's heart is a stream of water in the hand of the LORD; he turns it wherever he will."

The Lord turns the hearts of kings and the hearts of cupbearers. He makes them forget and He makes them remember.

That's because HE IS IN CONTROL.

The cupbearer would indeed turn out to be Joseph's get-out-of-jail-free card. But Joseph wouldn't hear a thing about it for two long years.

There's nothing more devastating than broken hopes. First your hopes are raised and then they are broken. It's happened to all of us.

## Out of Control

When our hopes are broken, it seems like our lives are completely out of control. There's no plan, no structure, and no organization. Nothing makes sense. When our hopes are broken, the glue in life is gone. Or so it seems.

Abraham Lincoln was a walking disaster. And no one knew it better than his law partner, William Herndon. Here's how Herndon described the man he worked with for years:

"He had no system, no order; he did not keep a clerk; he had neither library, nor index, nor cash-book. When he made notes, he would throw them into a drawer, put them in vest-pocket, or into his hat.... But in the inner man, a symmetry and method prevailed. He did not keep an orderly office, did not need pen and ink, because his workshop was in his head."[5]

When our hopes are broken, our lives can quickly fall apart. It seems to us that there is no system, no order, and no index to our lives. Nothing is on track or on schedule. But in the mind of God, those broken hopes contain a symmetry and method. God is at work in the midst of broken hopes. Broken hopes are just another tool in His workshop of providence.

God was the One who was behind the silence of the cupbearer. This had to be absolutely excruciating for Joseph. His one earthly hope was that the cupbearer would remember him. And it was on schedule to actually happen. But not until God gave him the nod.

David knew a lot about broken hopes. But he also knew the faithfulness of God. In Psalm 57:2–3, David was in serious trouble. He was surrounded by enemies, and destruction loomed over his head. These guys weren't making idle threats or playing games; they wanted to kill David. And here's what David says right in the midst of that life-threatening, heartbreaking situation:

> I will cry to God Most High,
> To God who accomplishes all things for me.
> He will send from heaven and save me.

One translator captures the sense of Psalm 57:2–3 this way:

> I will cry unto God most High,
> Unto God, the *transactor* of my affairs.
> He will send from heaven and save me.

## Taking Care of Business

You know what it's like to be involved in a business transaction. A transaction is a business deal that's either in the process of negotiation or already resolved. Now with that in mind, let's consider God as the transactor of your affairs. He is the One who accomplishes all things for you, who ultimately takes care of the business of your life. And even when you are in a situation like David, who was hiding in cave, or Joseph, who was stuck in prison on a bum rap, God is still taking care of the business of your life. You may be inactive, but God isn't. No matter where you are, God is the One who will see to the business of your life and who will accomplish all things for you.

Understand this: No matter how it may look to you in any given moment, the providence of God is *never* working against you. It is always working for you. Even when it seems that God has allowed your plans and your hopes to be crushed, He is not working against you.

That is His promise. That is the truth.

He is the transactor of all your affairs.

If you are in Christ, you know that He loves you so much that He sent His own Son to die for you. But you say, "I'm a great sinner." Yes, you are, and that's why He sent the Lord Jesus. He is *for* you, and as David said in Psalm 57:3, "He will send from heaven and save me."

He's about to send you help because He is the great transactor of your affairs.

When your hopes get dashed because of God's apparent silence, His plan for your life is still right on track. It can't be thwarted, and it can't be delayed. It can't be jammed or clogged or thrown off schedule. The workings of God for your life, the business of your life, God will get done. His plan is irresistible. No one, absolutely no one, can get in its way.

But we don't always see it this way, do we? We find ourselves in a cave of circumstances or a prison of disappointments, and the first thing we begin to do is question God or judge the way He is working. In fact, sometimes it seems like He isn't working at all, like He's on an extended leave or vacation, and we begin to murmur and complain.

We've all been there and experienced that attitude. Instead of thanking God and committing our path to Him, we begin to judge our circumstances too soon and call His goodness into account.

We begin to quickly indict God like an overeager district attorney indicting a college lacrosse team.

## Not So Elementary, My Dear Watson

Throughout this book, I have referred time and again to two Englishmen who lived in the 1600s: Thomas Watson and John Flavel. Watson wrote many books, but I have been reading his book *All Things for Good* for the last eight years. Not a week goes by that I don't pick it up. At the same time, I have also been reading through Flavel's *The Mystery of Providence* for the last eight years. I came across the two books in the same store on the same day, and I've been chewing on both of them ever since.

When it comes to the providence of God, both Watson and Flavel drive John Deere earthmovers. The subject is on every page in their writings. Now, they both were brilliant men, but they didn't write this stuff just to impress the boys at Oxford and Cambridge. They were living off these truths under unimaginable pressure and persecution.

Can you imagine what it would be like if the government suddenly declared that all pastors who preach the gospel of Christ must be immediately removed from their churches? That's actually what happened in England in 1662. The church and the state were the same at that time, so the king suddenly ordered the immediate removal of all conservative, Bible-believing pastors from their churches. They were no longer allowed to preach, and couldn't even come within five miles of a town. Immediately forfeiting their churches and their only means of support, these pastors were turned out of town without any provisions for them and their families. It was known as the Great Ejection.

Both Watson and Flavel were thrown out of their churches. Watson wrote the book *All Things for Good* to encourage his fellow pastors who were ejected from their churches.

John Flavel was one of those pastors who was ejected. His father was also a pastor and ejected. His father was then imprisoned and shortly thereafter died of the plague in 1665. John Flavel had to deal with the bitter pill of watching his father falsely imprisoned and impoverished. Not only that, but his own life was in constant danger. He was driven from his church, his home, and forced to live under the daily pressure of knowing that he could be arrested, tortured, and killed at any moment.

So when John Flavel writes his thoughts about not prejudging the works of God when they don't go our way, he knows firsthand of what he is speaking. This was no intellectual exercise with him. It was his life and his experience. He lived off the promises and the providence of God, and he knew that God was working in the midst of broken hopes. And Flavel had plenty of those. He knew the reality of broken hopes in his own life and in his own family.

Joseph had to deal with a broken hope when the cupbearer forgot him. But one day, two years in the future, the cupbearer would remember Joseph at the right time.

When something you are praying for is delayed, it doesn't necessarily mean God is saying no. He may be saying no for the time being—for a thousand reasons of which you have no conception. As it has so often been said, God's delays are not necessarily God's denials.

He is in control and He knows what He's doing even when our hopes are broken. And broken hopes are another link in the chain God is putting together for you and your children and their children—and even beyond.

## When the Godly Are Killed

When Steve Saint was five years old, he was hoping that his dad would get back from his trip into the jungle by dinnertime. But his dad didn't make it, and neither did the four other men who were with him deep in the rainforest of the Amazon. None of them ever came out of the jungle alive. They were speared to death on January 8, 1956, by the Auca Indians.

The Aucas were actually the Waodani tribe, but they were also known as Aucas, or "savage killers." Steve's hopes of seeing his father again were shattered. That's strong medicine for a five-year-old boy to swallow. Along with his mother, his aunt, and some of the other wives of the martyred missionaries, Steve actually lived among the men and their families who did the spearing.

It was the goodness of God that brought those murderers out of spiritual darkness and to the Lord. That's a great outcome, but it was still a broken hope for a five-year-old boy to lose his father in that way. It was nothing short of devastating. But fifty years later, in his remarkable book, *End of the Spear*, Steve offered his view of his broken hopes as he looked backward to that sad day.

> It is only my conjecture, because none of us can know the will of God, but I think it fit God's plan that all five men died. I know that might offend some who have a narrower opinion of the parameters within which God must operate, but I don't think what happened to my dad and his four friends caught God by surprise. Nor do I think that God simply allowed it. No, after learning in detail what happened on January 8, 1956—while I was so anxiously awaiting the speck of my

dad's little 56 Henry airplane over Penny Ridge—I believe God was much more involved in what happened than merely failing to intervene....

There are too many factors that all had to work together to have allowed the events to happen as they did. Too many for me to believe it was just chance. I have come to the conclusion that God did not look away. He did not simply allow this to happen. I think He planned it. Though this has not been an easy conclusion to come to, I believe it is the right one.

I have personally paid a high price for what happened on Palm Beach. But I have also had a front-row seat as the rest of the story has been unfolding for half a century. I have seen firsthand that much good has come from it. I believe only God could have fashioned such an incredible story from such a tragic event.

I could not begin to record the thousands of people who have told me that God used what happened on Palm Beach to change the course of their lives for good. Besides, it is enough for me that because Mincaye killed my father, my family now has the privilege of loving him and being loved by him. And because my dad and Jim and Ed and Peter and Roger were willing to die, Kimo and Dyuwi and Gikita and Ompodac and Tementa and Gaba and Odae and Tidi and Dawa and Cawaena and Coba and Gaacamo and their children and their grandchildren and their great-grandchildren and many others will all have a chance to live. If I could go back now and rewrite the script, I would not change a single scene. I have come to understand that life is too complex and much too short to let amateurs direct the story. I would rather let the Master Storyteller do the writing.[6]

Howard Head did not improve at tennis until he got a big racquet. You aren't going to get over the disappointment of your broken hopes until you understand that you need a BIG GOD.

And here's good news: You don't have to invent a BIG GOD for your life to improve. He is already there. He has always been and He will always be. He is the One who transacts all of your affairs and will accomplish that which concerns you. And in your broken hopes He will send from heaven and help you.

With no disrespect intended toward either sport, God has much, much more in mind for you than improving your skiing or tennis.

Chapter Seven

# Demoted and Benched

## He Is in Control ... Over Prolonged Waiting

*"I wait for the LORD, my soul does wait,*
*And in His word do I hope."*
—Psalm 130:5

Albert Einstein may have been a true genius, but like all graduate students, it still took him years of work to complete his doctor's dissertation. It was a great day for Einstein when he finally presented his paper, his dissertation for a PhD in physics, to his professor.

Several weeks later, he received the document back with a note. His dissertation had been rejected. The professor felt that the paper was too short.

It was a great disappointment to Einstein. A rejected dissertation could mean another year or two of plodding work. It would mean that he would have to wait for the degree, and then wait for the teaching jobs that required the degree.

There had to be a way around the waiting.

It was then that Einstein got his idea. He sat down and reread the entire dissertation. He then made one addition—but not another chapter and not another paragraph. In fact, he added *one sentence* to the paper, and turned it in once again.

It was promptly accepted, and Einstein somehow managed to avoid the long wait. Leave it to a genius to figure that out. But it usually doesn't work quite that well for the rest of us, with IQs below 180.

Waiting is like eating gravel. Nobody in their right mind wants to do it.

Why is that?

It's because none of us likes to wait—for anything.

Joseph had been thrown in jail on false charges. And now he was forced to wait. How long would it be before he was released—if at all? He had absolutely no idea. We know from the biblical account that Joseph was in the dungeon for two years, but he didn't know that. For all he knew, the years would grind on and on and he would die there.

When you're waiting in an Egyptian jail or in a prison of hard circumstances, there's not much you can do. And the longer you wait, the more discouraged you become.

Why doesn't God do something miraculous and instantly change our situations when we are waiting? I like the insight of Robert J. Morgan:

"Though miracles still occur, God uses them sparingly. Even in Scripture, miracles were not God's standard operating procedure. Many people assume the Bible is packed with miracles, but it isn't. Only during certain periods in biblical history were there clusterings of signs and wonders—during the Exodus, during the ministries of Elijah and Elisha, during the life of Christ and the early days of the apostles.

"Throughout most of the Bible, God helped His people in ordinary, providential ways rather than in overtly supernatural ones. The same is true today. That's why mature Christians pay special attention to the accidents, misfortunes, and coincidences that befall them. For in reality, there are no such things. Only the providential ordering of God who watches over His prayerful, trusting children, and whose unseen hand is guiding, guarding, arranging, and rearranging circumstances."[1]

We're sometimes compelled to wait in uncomfortable, uneasy circumstances where the outcome is far from certain. But even then—perhaps *especially* then—God is at work.

The prophet Isaiah makes that point clearly:

> No eye has seen a God besides you,
> who acts for those who wait for him.
> (Isa. 64:4 ESV)

When Joseph was in prison, God gave him the ability to interpret the dreams of the cupbearer and baker. That was miraculous. But other than that one miraculous intervention of God, Joseph waited. God gave him everything he needed while he was waiting, but God was slowly grinding the wheel of providence in Joseph's life on a daily basis. Joseph wasn't seeing miracles every day, but he was experiencing God's providence.

We tend to think that God works only through miracles. That's the error of the modern-day evangelical church. But God is *always* working. While we are waiting, God is working. He may not explain why He causes us to wait, but He doesn't have to. God knows exactly what He is doing.

Waiting is a large part of the Christian life. The concept of waiting on the Lord and His timing is everywhere in the Scriptures. But it's the last thing any of us ever wants to do. That gravel is hard on the teeth and murder to the digestive system!

Sometimes when we're waiting, we wonder why God is so slow in changing our situation. It just doesn't make any sense to us. We wait and wait and wait. And apparently, nothing is happening—and we get more and more frustrated.

## A Providential Purpose for Waiting

At a certain point in his life, the South African pastor Andrew Murray found himself in some very difficult and unwanted circumstances. As he was waiting for resolution, he made this notation in his journal:

Let me say I am here,

1. By God's appointment
2. In His keeping
3. Under His training
4. For His time.[2]

Those four observations were not only true in the life of Andrew Murray, they are true for you and me. And it's very apparent that they were true for Joseph. In fact, I'd like to borrow Murray's outline for this chapter on prolonged waiting.

## Joseph Waited by God's Appointment

As we have seen, Joseph had a divine appointment to become a virtual co-ruler with Pharaoh. But before he could attain that appointment, he was appointed to cool his heels in jail for two years. While he was in there, Joseph didn't know why he was there or how long he would be there. All he knew was that he was in a place he didn't want to be.

This is so often true of our experience. When we're in a prolonged season of waiting, we can see no good reason for it.

For many men, the trip of a lifetime would be a hunting or fishing expedition in the remote Alaskan wilderness. My friend Rocky McElveen has been an Alaskan guide and outfitter for thirty years. He has fulfilled the dreams of hundreds of men, including presidents of the United States, executives, ministry leaders, and their sons.[3]

As a result of living and guiding in the backcountry of this amazing state, Rocky has had enough life-threatening experiences to fill a hundred lifetimes. He's lived through plane crashes, grizzly attacks, and dangerous blizzards—and that was just one weekend (just kidding). He tells his remarkable experiences in his gripping book, *Wild Men, Wild Alaska*.

One of the most amazing stories he tells is about a group of hunters who had to wait. And they had no idea why. They were in the high backcountry, and one of the men, Ron, had just taken a huge trophy moose. Rocky had dressed out the moose, and the men in the hunting party had to pack out several hundred pounds of moose meat, along with the head and massive antlers of the moose, to the camp where they would meet the plane.

Now there's a slight problem that can develop when you're in the middle of the wild and remote wilderness. When a huge animal is dressed out, the scent of blood can be picked up for miles by wolves and grizzlies. Rocky writes,

> The pack would be horrendous. First we would have to traverse out of the valley, over tundra and creeks, through alders and brush, then a steep canyon and down another slippery slope to our camp and landing strip a couple of miles away. Each pack would be 150- to 200-plus pounds. I knew Jared needed help, so I decided to call in another packer, Jon, who is also my gourmet cook. I got on the phone to my pilot, Joel, and told him to fly Jon in and then me back out to the lodge.
>
> "I'll be back tomorrow," I told Ron when Joel and Jon arrived. "In the meantime, Joel can help you hunt for a bear or a wolf. If I were you, I would set up on the kill site."[4]

Rocky got in the plane and took off. It was September 10, 2001.

> Little did I know that by early morning the next day, no private planes would by flying anytime soon. Ron, Jared, and Jon would be on their own, without communication or supplies from anyone for days.[5]

The next morning was the attack on the World Trade Center and the Pentagon.

The FAA grounded all domestic planes indefinitely, including my plane. No guides or pilots in Alaska were able to fly and thus were powerless to check on the hundreds of hunters stranded in remote field camps. A fortunate few who could be reached by river or all-terrain vehicles were contacted and rescued.

One pilot friend of mine tried desperately to fly in supplies to a hunter he knew was low on water and food. He was forced down by military F-14 fighter planes.[6]

Rocky couldn't get to his hunters.

And they waited and waited and waited.

They didn't have a clue why Rocky hadn't shown up. The afternoon went by and then it got dark. Now they had to spend the night with hundreds of pounds of meat in bear and wolf country. The last thing they wanted was a visit from the wolves. And they certainly didn't need a grizzly coming around looking for a midnight snack. But both of those scenarios were very real possibilities.

Rocky didn't show up the next morning or the next afternoon. Once again darkness came. These guys had plenty to worry about. They had no ability to communicate, and they were hundreds of miles from the nearest town. They figured that Rocky had crashed in the plane. As they waited, the fear and worry increased. There was absolutely no explanation for their waiting. The longer they waited, the more they wondered if they would ever get out. The waiting made absolutely no sense to these stranded men.

Back at the lodge, Rocky called their families to let them know that the men had ample provisions, and that he would fly in to get them as soon as he could legally do so. On September 13, Rocky was able to finally send his pilot in to pick up the weary hunters.

When the plane landed one of the hunters vented his frustration on the pilot before he could even get out of the plane. *"Where have you been? Where's Rocky? He was supposed to finish the hunt with me!"*

The pilot quietly answered, "The United States has been attacked by terrorists."

At first the hunter thought that the pilot was kidding. But it only took a second to realize he was deadly serious.

Yes, they had been waiting in a very precarious and dangerous situation. But there was a very good reason for their waiting that they had known nothing about.

Later, one of the hunters wrote the following description to Rocky:

> I will never forget landing on the dirt runway behind the Holtna Lodge, taxiing up to the lodge, and seeing your bearded, smiling face as you greeted the plane. I got out of the plane, embraced you, and felt tremendous relief that we were all okay. You recapped the events as you understood them from 9/11 to 9/13. You told me it was the first time since the beginning of airplane flight in America that all flights had been halted nationwide for so long.
>
> I will always remember the next words you spoke to me. You looked up into the sky and said, "Ron, God is in control, not me. We may not understand these events, but God sees the past, present, and future, and He is in charge. We must trust Him."[7]

As far as those hunters were concerned, there was no good reason for their waiting. But there was a good reason—they just couldn't see it from their perspective. As they were waiting, so was Rocky. He knew very well why he was waiting, but that didn't change the situation. He still had to wait. Rocky had to wait knowing why; the hunters had to wait not knowing why.

If you're waiting for God to show up, maybe He's got some reasons, some very good reasons, for the delay. Actually there's no "maybe" about it. There are necessary reasons that you aren't privy to. So why not just give the frustration over to Him and trust that He knows best.

Go ahead.

Put down this book, bow your head, and give it over to Him. Tell Him what's on your heart. Get the anger out of your system, and then tell Him that you're willing to wait—even though you can't understand the reasons for it.

## Joseph Was in His Keeping

Joseph was sure that the cupbearer, with all his access to Pharaoh, would be the man to get him out of prison. And Joseph was right. The cupbearer would be the human instrument that God would use to bring Joseph to Pharaoh's attention. But Joseph thought it would happen right away—and it didn't. Joseph would watch the days drag by in that prison for two full years.

The entire time, however, the Lord was with Joseph. He was in the Lord's keeping.

When Rocky was forced to wait at the lodge for the stranded hunters, he did everything he could possibly do to make things ready for the men when the plane could finally retrieve them. But Rocky was waiting even as they were waiting. His hands were tied.

The Lord's hands are never tied. If the circumstances of our lives are tied up, it's because He has tied them up. It's by His appointment.

The hunters had no idea why they were waiting. But the United States of America had determined that it was in the best interests of national security to ground all aircraft. They were appointed to wait because of some very good reasons they had no way of knowing or conceiving. It was no mistake that they were waiting.

When God appoints us to wait, it baffles us. Prolonged waiting makes no sense! But it's all under control. Your waiting is no mistake. A. M. Overton captured this so well many years ago in his poem "He Maketh No Mistake":

> My Father's way may twist and turn,
> My heart may throb and ache,
> But in my soul I'm glad to know,
> He maketh no mistake.

My cherished plans may go astray,
My hopes may fade away,
But I'll trust my Lord to lead,
For He doth know the way.

Tho' night be dark, and it may seem
That day will never break,
I'll pin my faith, my all in Him,
He maketh no mistake.

There's so much now I cannot see,
My eyesight's far too dim;
But come what may, I'll simply trust,
And leave it all to Him.

For by and by the mist will lift
And plain it all He'll make,
Through all the way, tho' dark to me
He made not one mistake.

If you are in the place of prolonged waiting, it is no mistake. He will keep you and He will carry you during your time of waiting on Him … and far beyond that. He carries us, provides for us, and sustains us throughout our lifetimes on this earth. Check out these verses and you will see it in black and white:

Save Your people and bless Your inheritance;
Be their shepherd also, and *carry them forever.*
(Ps. 28:9)

For such is God,
Our God forever and ever;

He will guide us until death.
(Ps. 48:14)

Listen to Me, O house of Jacob,
And all the remnant of the house of Israel,
You who have been borne by Me from birth
And have been carried from the womb;
Even to your old age I will be the same,
And even to your graying years I will bear you!
I have done it, and I will carry you;
And I will bear you and I will deliver you.
(Isa. 46:3–4)

Now that's what you call a promise. And Congress can't take it away.

Thomas Watson was correct when he penned these words: "The care of Providence runs parallel with the line of life."

## Joseph Waited Under His Training

If God calls you to wait, it is imperative that you do so. It is part of our training that prepares us for the work God has for us to do. Joseph was being trained in prison while he waited. He had to *learn* to wait on God for His timing.

Now let's clarify something quickly. There is waiting and there is waiting—and *waiting* in the pages of Scripture is not about some guy being lazy and a sluggard. It's not about sitting on your tail all day and not taking care of business. It's not an excuse to be passive. It's not counting flowers on the wall and playing solitaire till dawn. We're talking about situations where God puts you in a hard place and makes you wait for His answer to your dilemma. In the meantime, you go about your business and take the bull by the horns as much as you legitimately can.

From all that we can see in Scripture, Joseph was willing to wait it out and tough it out. You never read one word about him complaining to the Lord or becoming bitter. He was willing, as 1 Peter 4:19 states, to "entrust [his soul] to a faithful Creator in doing what is right."

Waiting is an exercise of faith that demonstrates the condition of our hearts. Waiting on God is an act of faith. And faith is what separates the men from the boys.

Saul and David, the first two kings of Israel, give us a clear contrast in their responses to a situation of forced waiting. There was a huge difference between these two men. One was willing to wait on God and the other wasn't. One was willing to be trained (David) and the other wasn't (Saul). And as a result, Saul started strong, but he didn't finish strong.

Saul was the tallest man is Israel—but he was a wuss. Because he didn't have the guts to wait. The context here is that the Philistines had a massive army coming up against Israel, their long-time enemy. Panicking, the people literally began to hide themselves in the rocks from the invading army. Seeing this, Saul's faith melted faster than an ice sculpture in a sauna. Instead of waiting on the Lord for the appointed time established by Samuel the prophet, Saul went into his panic mode and took matters into his own hands.

Let me just say this: Taking matters out of God's hands and putting them in your own hands is never a good policy. In fact, it's a train wreck.

> When the men of Israel saw that they were in a strait (for the people were hard-pressed), then the people hid themselves in caves, in thickets, in cliffs, in cellars, and in pits. Also some of the Hebrews crossed the Jordan into the land of Gad and Gilead. But as for Saul, he was still in Gilgal, and all the people followed him trembling.
>
> Now he waited seven days, according to the appointed time set by Samuel, but Samuel did not come to Gilgal; and the people were scattering from him. So Saul said, "Bring to me the burnt offering and the peace offerings." And he offered the burnt offering. As soon

as he finished offering the burnt offering, behold, Samuel came; and Saul went out to meet him and to greet him. But Samuel said, "What have you done?" And Saul said, "Because I saw that the people were scattering from me, and that you did not come within the appointed days, and that the Philistines were assembling at Michmash, therefore I said, 'Now the Philistines will come down against me at Gilgal, and I have not asked the favor of the LORD.' So I forced myself and offered the burnt offering." Samuel said to Saul, "You have acted foolishly; you have not kept the commandment of the LORD your God, which He commanded you, for now the LORD would have established your kingdom over Israel forever. But now your kingdom shall not endure. The LORD has sought out for Himself a man after His own heart, and the LORD has appointed him as ruler over His people, because you have not kept what the LORD commanded you." (1 Sam. 13:6–14)

The Lord was looking for a man after His own heart. Saul was not the man. Rather than waiting on God, Saul impatiently took matters into his own hands, and did what he had clearly been told not to do. Saul's unwillingness to wait was a clear-cut lack of obedience.

Interesting, isn't it, that when God looks for a man after His own heart, the test of that man's heart is his willingness to wait?

Saul was unwilling to wait. And he lost the kingdom that could have been his for generations. Resisting God's training, he just didn't have the heart to obey.

## Joseph Was Waiting for His Time

God is the great Timekeeper of our times of prolonged waiting.

That is the clear statement that David made in Psalm 31:15: *"My times are in Your hand."*

Going into his two-year stint of prolonged waiting, Joseph had no idea how long he would be in that mode. The Lord had determined two years, and two years it was.

I have had four seasons of prolonged waiting in my life.

The first was in my early twenties and it lasted about eighteen months. The second was in my midtwenties and it lasted twelve months. The third was in my early thirties and this one ran about three years. The fourth was in my late thirties and it lasted four years.

That's a lot of waiting.

I can assure you that I wasn't just sitting around. I earned two degrees, found a wife, and had three children. I also pastored in three different churches. But at the same time, God had me doing some significant waiting as He trained me for a work that I knew nothing about.

Briefly, I'd like to relate to you my shortest experience of prolonged waiting, which lasted about a year.


## Waiting for a Green Light

As a student in seminary, I worked on the truck docks at night in order to pay my way through school. It was a part-time job of four hours a night that enabled me to take a full load of classes and still have time to study.

But then a national recession hit and my part-time job was eliminated. For weeks I looked for work, and it was as though every job for a hundred miles had dried up. Companies were laying off workers right and left. It looked like I would have to leave school, go home to California, and just work for a year to save money to finish out seminary. That appeared to be my only option.

Then one of my friends who knew my situation said, "Steve, are you familiar with the XYZ Corporation?" Now that wasn't the real name of the company, but it will be for this story. The company that he named was the largest employer in the state and one of the fifty largest companies in America. The corporate skyscraper was the largest building in the entire state.

My friend went on to tell me that the president of the company was a family friend. He had known this gentleman since he was in first grade and they were on a first-name basis. And then he told me that he had set up an appointment the next afternoon in the president's office. I couldn't believe it. It turned out that this man was a committed Christian who had been very supportive of the seminary that I attended. When my friend mentioned my situation and that I was being forced to leave seminary, the man suggested that I come in and talk with him.

Entering this majestic office overlooking the entire city, I was more than a little intimidated. But this fine gentleman was very warm and asked me to tell him my situation. After several minutes of my bringing him up to date, he smiled and said, "Well, Steve, it seems to me that the best course would be for you to stay and finish out seminary without taking a year off. Let me call my vice president of human resources and talk with him. I'm sure we can find some kind of work to help you finish out school. Could you come back tomorrow afternoon?"

I indicated that I could. Here was the biggest employer in the state going to bat for me. I will tell you that my hopes were suddenly raised. When I told my friend what happened, he said, "I'm sure by this time tomorrow you'll have a new job—and if not, this gentleman has a multimillion-dollar foundation that gives educational grants. One way or the other, he's going to make sure that you finish seminary without going back to California." My hopes were soaring after that piece of news.

The next afternoon I walked into this man's office at four o'clock. Instead of being warm and friendly, however, he actually seemed somewhat distant and stiff. He then said, "Steve, I'm sorry but I have no job to offer you. I wish things could have worked out differently. I thank you for coming in." And then he stood up and the appointment was over.

I have to tell you that I was a little shell-shocked—not so much about the job as by the man's approach. It was almost cold. It really took me aback. I was scrambling in my mind to think through our previous interview. *Had I done something wrong? Had I said something inappropriate?* I couldn't think of a thing.

"I thank you for checking on the job possibilities," I said as I stood to leave the room. "I completely understand. But before I leave, may I clarify something? I came back in this afternoon because you asked me to come back."

"Yes, that's correct. I thank you for coming."

The reason I wanted to clarify that he had asked me come back was that his demeanor was so radically different than the previous day. It was so different that I thought I had somehow offended him. I shook his hand and walked out of the massive office and got on the elevator. As I was walking to my car, I remember saying, "Lord, that was such an extreme shift in that man's response that it had to be from You."

And at that moment, I knew that was my last shot at staying in school. I went back to my room, started packing, and left for home the next morning.

## Another Round of Waiting

At least, I told myself, I could get work on the truck docks in San Jose. But what I didn't know was that jobs were just as tight in California. And for the next six months, I waited. I talked to every foreman at every company I could find. I had all kinds of experience. But for three months nothing happened.

Finally, one foreman called and said he could use me one night a week. That was better than nothing, but it wasn't much. I was living at home and I felt like a failure. I was twenty-five and going nowhere! My friends were back in seminary taking classes and making their way forward to graduation. And what was I doing? I was sitting. Well, I wasn't just sitting because I spent so much time filling out job applications. But everyone told me that they weren't hiring, so filling out applications all day was a waste of time.

I can't tell you how frustrated I was. It was like the Lord had put me on hold. I was doing everything I could do to find work, but there was absolutely nothing out there. Not even McDonald's was hiring! I wasn't going to school, I wasn't working, and I wasn't saving money so I could get back to seminary. One night a week was all I could get.

So in my down time I read. Then I read some more. And then I read more books that I wanted to read when I was in seminary but didn't have time with the required reading and with work. During that time, I read over forty books that I had wanted to read but never quite got to. Now I got to them. This went on for six months.

Then one night the foreman came up to me and said, "Steve, I've got an opening starting in three weeks on the graveyard shift. If you can handle working all night, you've got the job."

*"I'll take it!"* was my subtle response.

Finally the waiting was over, and I was pumped. After months of not doing anything (except reading some very important books that have impacted me to this day), I finally had a job. And with the good hourly wage, I knew that I could save enough to go back to seminary and finish out.

The waiting was over and my next step was clear.

Or at least I thought it was.

But it all changed when I went to church on Sunday night. I showed up at Peninsula Bible Church in Palo Alto, California. It was packed as usual with college students, singles, and families. In this service, there was great music and excellent teaching, usually from Ray Stedman, David Roper, or Ron Ritchie.

But there was something they always did.

They always took about twenty minutes to have an open mike. If people had prayer requests or needs or something to share from Scripture, during the "Body Life" time, they could raise their hand, and when they were recognized, they would be handed a microphone. It was always very interesting because it wasn't scripted.

On this particular evening, the sharing was somewhat heavy. Everyone who shared was carrying a heavy burden. As I was listening to this, I thought that it might be an encouragement for everyone to hear an *answer* to prayer. Just as the sharing time was coming to an end, I raised my hand and Ron

Ritchie caught my eye. The next thing I knew I had a mike in my hand, and in about two minutes I told my story of coming home from seminary and doing nothing but waiting. But the good news was that I would finally have a full-time job in three weeks.

## A Last-Minute Curveball

When the service was over, a guy walked right up to me and introduced himself. He said that he thought we'd met somewhere. He told me where he was from, and I responded that I had been in that town only once in my life. I was at a church with a music group that I sang with in college.

He said he'd been the youth pastor of that church back then, and now he was the pastor. He was a sharp-looking guy in his thirties. As we briefly talked, we discovered we had some mutual friends. He then asked if I had time to get some coffee.

At the coffee shop I asked him what brought him to California. He said, "I'm looking for someone to help me pastor this church. We've been through a big transition." He then told me that they had been in a certain denomination, but had moved out of it because they were realizing that some of the teaching had been overemphasized.

I knew that denomination, because I had been raised in it—and I had come to the same conclusions. As we talked, he asked me about my background and what I was doing. I told him my story and that I was finally going to work full-time so I could go back and finish seminary.

After several minutes he said, "I think you're the guy I'm looking for. Why don't you come and help me with this church?"

I thought he was nuts. After all, I had to work full-time and save my money so I could return and finish seminary. He asked how much I would make unloading trucks. I told him the amount, and he said that they could probably pay me the same amount.

"But I'm going back in six months to school!" I told him. "You don't want someone for six months!"

With a smile, he replied that six months just might work out to help them get established with the transition.

This was the craziest thing I had ever heard. Three days later he called and invited me to come down for the weekend. He had talked with the men on the board, and they said they'd like to meet me. I told him that I really thought it would be a waste of their money and time to bring me down. It just didn't fit into my plans.

"Well," he said, "what else are you doing this weekend?"

He had me. I had nothing at all going that weekend, and no excuse for not making the trip with him. So I reluctantly went.

Here's the upshot of the story. After six months of waiting, on the day that I should have started my new job on the truck docks, I was driving my car to a town in another state to begin a six-month pastorate. In that six months, I learned all kinds of practical things about leading a growing church in transition. At the end of that half-year assignment, I went back to finish seminary with hands-on experience for ministry that I never would have gotten on the truck docks.

Little did I know that just three years after that, I would be called to pastor a small church that was in major transition. Without that six months of practical experience under my belt, I would have been in over my head. Well … I actually was *still* in over my head. But the prior experience had given me a huge education that helped me deal with the issues I now faced.

Looking back, the twelve-month hiatus from school makes all kinds of sense. When I was in the middle of it, it made no sense. When I was invited to work in the church, I enjoyed the six months very much. I made some lasting friendships and soaked up knowledge and experience like never before. But I still wanted to get back to seminary.

During my twelve months of waiting, I had been more than ready for God to step on the accelerator—but He wouldn't take His foot off the brake! That brought a lot of frustration into my life. In my immaturity, I had very little peace and very little joy.

Jeremiah had to fight the same kind of battle:

> My soul has been rejected from peace;
> I have forgotten happiness.
> So I say, "My strength has perished.
> And so has my hope from the LORD....
> This I recall to mind,
> Therefore I have hope,
> The LORD's lovingkindnesses indeed never cease,
> For His compassions never fail.
> They are new every morning;
> Great is Your faithfulness....
> The LORD is good to those who wait for Him,
> To the person who seeks Him.
> It is good that he waits silently
> For the salvation of the LORD.
> (Lam. 3:17–18, 21–23, 25–26)

## Summing It All Up

Waiting is easy to write about. But it's hard to live out. Maybe that's why, even as I've been writing this chapter, I have been waiting. I thought the answer to the promise would have arrived months and months ago. But it hasn't.

In the middle of writing this chapter, I had to take a week off because I was wrestling in my own heart with the difficulty of God's timing. I understand prolonged waiting in my head—but it has to get into my heart. When all else fails, I can only go back to the Scriptures.

Did you catch that line in Lamentations 3—"the LORD is good to those who wait for Him"? I've counted on that verse before and I'm counting on it again. And for some reason, I have the distinct impression that I'm not alone.

The previous chapter spoke about broken hopes, and this one has been about prolonged waiting. The two are linked together. The fact of the matter is that the longer we wait, the more we struggle with broken hopes.

What's the solution? It is found in Psalm 130:5:

> I wait for the LORD, my soul does wait,
> And in His word do I hope.

There it is. That's the answer. If you are waiting on God, the only way that you keep hope alive is to stay in your Bible. Read it, chew on it, and embrace the promises. Do the work that God has laid before you to do. Take whatever legitimate steps you can take to improve your situation. But as you do so and as you continue to wait for God to come through, whatever you do, don't close your Bible and stick it on the shelf. If you do that, you've just closed the door on your source of hope.

Keep your Bible open and live off the promises. God will come through. And when He does, you'll agree that it was worth the wait. And in the meantime, don't forget:

You are waiting,
1. By God's appointment
2. In His keeping
3. Under His training
4. For His time.[8]

He's got it all under control.

Even if you're one sentence short.

## Chapter Eight

# Powerful Punks

## He Is in Control …
## Over Powerful People

*"God is the cause of causes."*
*—Christopher Nesse*

I was over at Barnes and Noble last week and I picked up two books: *MoonPie: Biography of an Out-of-This-World Snack* by David Magee, and *God Is Not Great* by Christopher Hitchens.

*MoonPie* was the better book hands down.

If you have ever had the privilege of eating a MoonPie and washing it down with an RC Cola, you know that you have just experienced a merciful providence.

Regarding that second book … I have appreciated Hitchens' willingness over the years to tell the unvarnished truth when it comes to world affairs. But he comes unhinged when it comes to Christianity and religion in general. He had some legitimate gripes about various religious teachings and practices.

But he crosses the line when he mocks the One True God. He writes the following blurb:

> Imagine that you can a perform a feat of which I am incapable. Imagine, in other words, that you can picture an infinitely

benign and all-powerful creator, who conceived of you, then made and shaped you, brought you into the world that he had made for you, and now supervises and cares for you even while you sleep.[1]

That's not hard for me to imagine.

That's the story of my life and yours.

It's the most comforting thing in all the world to know that there is a God who is in charge of my life.

Hitchens is to be pitied.

The God of the Bible *is* great. And not only is He great, He is in control of everything, including powerful people.

## A Bad Rap

Pharaoh was the most powerful man on the face of the earth. He had every luxury and privilege imaginable. (Except for the MoonPies. He missed out on those by somewhere around twenty-nine hundred years.)

Joseph was in Pharaoh's prison.

I'm not in prison.

But I know a man who is in prison. He comes from a fine Christian family, has an excellent education, and is the last person you would ever expect to be in jail.

Everyone familiar with his case agrees on one thing: He should not be behind bars. I won't go into the details of the case except to say this: He was charged, along with a number of individuals, in a case of white-collar crime. The others were charged with much more serious offenses. But everyone, including the prosecuting attorney, agreed that he should not be doing jail time.

But he is.

After several years of fighting the charges, and spending virtually every dime that he had, this man decided to accept a plea bargain. He would do no jail time and the whole incident would be put behind him. But after the agreement was made, he got a call and found out he was going to jail. Someone with some power had stepped in and nixed the agreement.

So, two weeks after his first child was born, he checked into a federal prison to do time for a crime he didn't commit, to do time that he didn't deserve. This man is a Christian, and he's been part of a Bible study I teach for several years.

So how does that mesh with the concept that God is in control of powerful people? The case is on appeal, but by the time it will be heard, the man will have served his sentence.

Someone with a lot of power overruled the plea bargain.

But God is in control of powerful people.

Does that make any sense?

## The King of Kings and the Judge of Judges

Jesus is the King of Kings.

He is also the controller of kings and all powerful people.

Including your boss. And including all judges.

Remember Proverbs 21:1?

> The king's heart is like channels of water
> in the hand of the LORD;
> He turns wherever He wishes.

That also goes for prime ministers, presidents, CEOs, and military dictators. It applies to college presidents, police chiefs, and school-board members. Anyone anywhere who has a position of authority is under control of the King of Kings. Anyone who breathes—He controls (Isa. 42:5). He's in control of powerful people, weak people, and everyone in between.

Jerry Bridges is correct: "God rules as surely on earth as He does in Heaven. For reasons known only to Himself, God permits people to act contrary to and in defiance of His revealed will in the Bible."[2]

But He is still in control over powerful people.

God owns them, runs them, and uses them for His purpose. And they do precisely what He ordains. That's quite a statement about His power over the kings of the earth: He takes their hearts and turns them, like channels of water, in whatever way He so wishes.

Not all Christians believe this. Not all pastors believe this clear teaching of Scripture. One pastor has questions about the power of God over powerful people: "God simply can't override free wills whenever they might conflict with His will. Because God decided to create this kind of world, He can't ensure that His will is carried out in every situation. He must tolerate and wisely work around the irrevocable freedom of human and spirit agents."[3]

So ... we're to understand that powerful men apparently have more power than God? They can do anything they want and God can't?

Proverbs 21:1 states that God most certainly does override free wills, and He does so whenever He chooses. There are many other verses that teach the same concept. King Nebuchadnezzar comes to mind in Daniel 4. In his day, he was the most powerful man on the face of the earth. Should it surprise any of us that all the bowing, pampering, and adulation he had enjoyed since earliest memory went to his head a little?

By the time he assumed the reins of power in Babylon, he was on an interstellar ego trip. He didn't think God was great, he thought *he* was great. So after a warning from Daniel that he ignored, one year later God gave him the mind of an animal. For the next seven years he grazed out in the fields with the Angus. And at the end of the seven years, God gave him his mind back. And now he had a very strong inclination to say that God was great.

But according to the teacher I quoted above, humans have irrevocable free will, and so do spirit agents. By spirit agents, I assume he means angels and demons (who are fallen angels). So let me get this straight … this teacher is asserting that the will of a human or the will of an angel trumps the will of God.

How can a human have irrevocable free will and God doesn't? Romans 9:16 says that "it does not depend on the man who wills … but on God who has mercy."

With this kind of weak teaching, no wonder we tend to think that powerful people are in control. But if we believe that, we're badly mistaken. *God controls powerful people.* They are at His beck and call, and they serve Him 24/7. They serve Him even if they are in rebellion to Him. They breathe because He allows them to breathe, and they think because He permits them to think (just ask Nebuchadnezzar). He can take away their ability to think and reason in an instant.

As we have seen, when leaders or presidents sin, they are responsible for their sin. God is never the author of sin because of His absolute holiness. But He uses powerful people for His purposes, and ultimately uses them for His glory and the good of His people.

When we come to Genesis 41, we're introduced to a pharaoh who was the most powerful man on earth at that time. He had a dream, Joseph interpreted that dream, and Pharaoh subsequently appointed him to a post of virtual co-leadership of Egypt.

Joseph became the most powerful man in Egypt—and thereby one of the most powerful men on the planet. All of this came about because the Lord turned Pharaoh's heart to accomplish the will of heaven. And it all began with a dream that God made him dream. Pharaoh had no option to refuse this dream. God sent it special delivery into the king's subconscious in the middle of the night and that was that.

Basically, God said to this powerful king, "Dream *this*, you little Egyptian wuss."

## Why Pharaoh Had Power

Although he never held an elective office, Robert Moses was the most powerful man in the history of the state of New York. He had more power than any governor, including Franklin Delano Roosevelt, who served in that position from 1928 to 1932. Most people outside of New York have never heard of Robert Moses. Yet he was probably the most brilliant and powerful bureaucrat that America ever produced. Moses reigned and ruled over the public agencies that built roads, bridges, parks, and housing projects. "He developed a political machine that virtually became a fourth branch of government," according to Robert Caro's monumental biography, *The Power Broker.* "Moses built an empire and lived like an emperor. He was the greatest builder that the world has ever seen."[4]

How did Robert Moses get into such a powerful position? He managed, time and time again, to write massive bills for state representatives who never read the fine print. They handed power over to Moses that made him the virtual dictator of New York for close to four decades. He literally reshaped New York City during that time. But ultimately, he had power because God used him for His purposes.

Before we look at Pharaoh's dream, we should consider *why* he was the king of Egypt. How did he get that position in the first place? The superficial answer would be that his father was Pharaoh, and upon his death, the title and position were conveyed upon him as the firstborn son. But there's more to it than just family succession.

Our sovereign God is the One who raises men and women to prominence and power, and just as quickly removes them. As Mary, the mother of Jesus, said in her Magnificat,

> He has done mighty deeds with His arm;
> He has scattered those who were proud in the thoughts of
> their heart.

He has brought down rulers from their thrones,

And has exalted those who were humble.

(Luke 1:51–52)

Some two thousand years before Mary, the prophet Isaiah had a startling vision of the greatness of God compared to our concepts of earthly greatness. In this magnificent chapter, God invites us to take things and people we believe to be mighty and imposing and compare them to Him. When we do that, we gain perspective very quickly. In Isaiah 40:18, God asks the question, "To whom then will you liken Me?"

I would suggest you read the following verses very slowly, allowing yourself time to taste and savor the greatness of our God. Consider carefully His unlimited power:

Who has measured the waters in the hollow of His hand,

And marked off the heavens by the span,

And calculated the dust of the earth by the measure,

And weighed the mountains in a balance

And the hills in a pair of scales?

Who has directed the Spirit of the LORD,

Or as His counselor has informed Him?

With whom did He consult and who gave Him understanding?

And who taught Him in the path of justice and taught Him knowledge

And informed Him of the way of understanding?

Behold, the nations are like a drop from a bucket,

And are regarded as a speck of dust on the scales;

Behold, He lifts up the islands like fine dust.

Even Lebanon is not enough to burn,

Nor its beasts enough for a burnt offering.

All the nations are as nothing before Him,

They are regarded by Him as less than nothing and meaningless.
(Isa. 40:12–17)

In Joseph's time, Egypt was the world's superpower, the big bad boy on the block. Every other nation feared Egypt and their military might. But eventually the rule of Egypt ran its course and they became a minor country with minor influence. (See Ezek. 29—32.)

Many historians have written about the rise and fall of great nations, the most famous being Arnold Toynbee, who wrote twelve volumes around the subject.

Sir John Glubb wrote an essay in 1976 titled "The Fate of Empires." Glubb put forth his theory that great empires rarely survive more than 250 years.[5]

Why do these empires fall? Sir John suggests numerous reasons. But the ultimate reason emblazoned across the pages of Scripture is that God brings them down. God is in control of powerful nations and powerful leaders ... including every single one of the empires listed below.

| The Nation | Dates | Time in Years |
| --- | --- | --- |
| Assyria | 859–612 BC | 247 |
| Persia | 538–330 BC | 208 |
| Greece | 331–100 BC | 231 |
| Roman Republic | 260–27 BC | 233 |
| Roman Empire | 27 BC–AD 180 | 207 |
| Arab Empire | AD 634–880 | 246 |
| Mameluke Empire | 1250–1517 | 267 |
| Ottoman Empire | 1320–1517 | 250 |
| Spain | 1500–1750 | 250 |
| Romanov Russia | 1682–1916 | 234 |
| Britain | 1700–1950 | 250[6] |

It was Winston Churchill who said, "The farther backward you can look, the farther forward you are likely to see."

So what nations are feared today? Obviously the United States of America. But many people have trouble sleeping at night when they think about the nuclear capabilities of Iran and North Korea. Yet in the verses we just read, God says all the nations are as *nothing* before Him. In fact, they are less than nothing and meaningless. So instead of worrying about nuclear war tonight, why don't you simply read Isaiah 40 before you go to sleep? Red China, Iraq, the Taliban, Hezbollah, and Hamas, and other terrorists organizations fall directly under His sovereign control.

They are nothing. They are meaningless.

Can they do evil and harm? Of course they can. But they cannot touch the life of a believer without the consent of God. He controls them and He runs them—powerful nations and terrorist groups as well. And here's what these terrorist organizations probably don't realize: God, *the true and living God,* appoints their leaders and sets the length of their term. And when He is finished with them, He blows on them and they wither.

That's what you call power.

> Do you not know? Have you not heard?
> Has it not been declared to you from the beginning?
> Have you not understood from the foundations of the earth?
> It is He who sits above the circle of the earth,
> And its inhabitants are like grasshoppers,
> Who stretches out the heavens like a curtain
> And spreads them out like a tent to dwell in.
> He it is who reduces rulers to nothing,
> Who makes the judges of the earth meaningless.
> Scarcely have they been planted,
> Scarcely have they been sown,
> Scarcely has their stock taken root in the earth,

But He merely blows on them, and they wither,
And the storm carries them away like stubble.
"To whom then will you liken Me
That I would be his equal?" says the Holy One.
Lift up your eyes on high
And see who has created these stars,
The One who leads forth their host by number,
He calls them all by name;
Because of the greatness of His might and the strength of His
power,
Not one of them is missing.
(Isa. 40:21–26)

Great leaders build palaces. God builds solar systems by speaking them into instantaneous existence.

Teddy Roosevelt was one of our greatest presidents. He was used to power and comfortable in using it. But he understood full well where real power came from. As he confessed to his friends, "After a week of wrestling with perplexing problems, it does so rest my soul to come into the house of the Lord and to sing—and to mean it—Holy, Holy, Holy, Lord God Almighty."[7]

It is no wonder, then, that "often before retiring to bed, Roosevelt, and naturalist friend William Beebe, would step outside the White House and look up into the night sky, searching for a tiny patch of light near the constellation Pegasus.

"'That is the Spiral Galaxy in Andromeda,' they would chant in unison. 'It is as large as our Milky Way. It is one of a hundred million galaxies. It consists of one hundred billions suns, each larger than our own sun.'

"After a moment of silent awe, Roosevelt would then turn to his companion and say, 'Now I think we are small enough. Let's go to bed.'"[8]

President Theodore Roosevelt was a powerful man with a big ego. But he kept that ego in check by making sure he dressed his eyes with salve and looked up to the stars. And he knew full well that the One who created those stars was not only all-powerful, but infinitely holy.

Not all powerful people like to acknowledge anyone greater than themselves. But from time to time they are reminded that their sum total is a big, hollow zero.

So why was Pharaoh a mighty ruler in the world during the lifetime of Joseph? The answer is simply that God put him there. God raises up rulers and He sets them down. When He blows on them, they melt away to nothing like the Wicked Witch of the West in the *Wizard of Oz*. It is God who reduces rulers to nothing and makes the judges of the earth meaningless. First God declared that the nations are meaningless, and now He states that judges and other powerful people are meaningless as well.

Then He commands, "Lift up your eyes on high and see who created these stars!"

Powerful people like to ponder their own greatness when, in fact, they are nothing and meaningless. The only reason that they hold a position of authority at all is because God placed them there for a season of time ordained by Him for His purposes and His glory. That's why Pharaoh was the king of Egypt.

And now, in Genesis 41, God is about to reach right through all of this king's elaborate defenses and security cordon, and plant a dream in the middle of his subconscious.

## Pleasant and Unpleasant Dreams

When does Pharaoh have this life-changing, world-shaping dream of his?

When he is asleep, of course.

It was Heraclitus who observed that "even sleepers are workers and collaborators in what goes on in the universe." That's true, and it's all because God runs the universe.

Pharaoh was about to cooperate with the plan of God simply because he needed to get some sleep.

But that's a hint right there that he really wasn't all that powerful. If you have to sleep every night, then you really aren't much when it comes to power. By the way, we should point out that back in Isaiah 40:28, a point is made about the power of God.

> Do you not know? Have you not heard?
> *The Everlasting God, the LORD, the Creator of the ends of the earth*
> *Does not become weary or tired.*

God never sleeps. He never nods off. He never needs to grab a quick power nap in the afternoon. He doesn't need sleep because He never, ever loses energy. That's what you call power.

But Pharaoh, whom everyone feared and thought so mighty and awesome, had to go to bed. Nine or ten o'clock came around, and he started yawning and slouching on that throne of his. So he put on his silk pajamas and crawled into his three-hundred-count Egyptian Pima cotton sheets to go to sleep. And here's what happened as recorded in Genesis 41:1–8 (ESV):

> After two whole years, Pharaoh dreamed that he was standing by the Nile, and behold, there came up out of the Nile seven cows attractive and plump, and they fed in the reed grass. And behold, seven other cows, ugly and thin, came up out of the Nile after them, and stood by the other cows on the bank of the Nile. And the ugly, thin cows ate up the seven attractive, plump cows. And Pharaoh awoke. And he fell asleep and dreamed a second time. And behold, seven ears of grain, plump and good, were growing on one stalk. And behold, after them sprouted seven ears, thin and blighted by the east

wind. And the thin ears swallowed up the seven plump, full
ears. And Pharaoh awoke, and behold, it was a dream. So in
the morning his spirit was troubled, and he sent and called
for all the magicians of Egypt and all its wise men. Pharaoh
told them his dreams, but there was none who could interpret
them to Pharaoh.

It was one of those dreams where you wake up and feel troubled, with the
images still dancing across the screen of your mind. Pharaoh woke up and was
really disturbed by this fat-cow, skinny-cow dream. It may be that he realized
there was something unusual, something significant, about the dream—and
not just a result of eating too many barbequed frog legs the night before.

Trying to shake off that uneasy feeling, he probably told himself, "Relax,
it's just a dream," rolled over, and went back to sleep.

But then he had a second dream—this time, involving ears of grain. First,
they were full and robust, and then they withered. Once again he woke up and
realized he'd been dreaming. But he couldn't blow off those dreams. He was
troubled by them, because he knew they meant something. So he called all of his
wise men and intellectuals together for an early morning meeting, so that they
could interpret the dream. (Why else would you keep a bunch of wise men on
the payroll?) These guys went to Harvard, Yale, and Oxford—or the Egyptian
equivalents—but when it came to dreams, they were clueless. That's because this
dream came from God, and the things of God are spiritually discerned.

It would take a man who knew God to interpret a God-sent dream. And
that's about the time the royal cupbearer remembered an extraordinary young
Hebrew down in Pharaoh's dungeons.

Then the chief cupbearer said to Pharaoh, "I remember my
offenses today. When Pharaoh was angry with his servants
and put me and the chief baker in custody in the house of the
captain of the guard, we dreamed on the same night, he and

I, each having a dream with its own interpretation. A young
Hebrew was there with us, a servant of the captain of the
guard. When we told him, he interpreted our dreams to us,
giving an interpretation to each man according to his dream.
And as he interpreted to us, so it came about. I was restored to
my office, and the baker was hanged." (vv. 9–13 ESV)

That was all Pharaoh needed to hear. His advisors were standing around
bug-eyed, like deer caught in the headlights—and absolutely worthless to their
king.

Check this out: At this precise moment the most powerful man on earth
was reminded that he was out of power. He did not have the power to figure
out his dilemma.

But watch the power of God now kick into gear.

Suddenly a lightbulb lit up over the cupbearer's head. How could he have
forgotten? There was a man in prison who could do precisely what Pharaoh
needed.

And what did Pharaoh need? He needed a man who could interpret dreams
accurately. He wasn't looking for someone who would take a wild stab at an
interpretation or try to flatter the boss with a politically correct pleasantry.
Something had stirred Pharaoh to the soul, and he needed the real deal—
someone who could proclaim his troubling dream and explain it in detail.

Pharaoh sent and called Joseph, and they quickly brought him
out of the pit. And when he had shaved himself and changed
his clothes, he came in before Pharaoh. (v. 14 ESV)

The providence of God had been preparing for years the young man
who was about to be handed the reins of power in Egypt—by Pharaoh
himself. It's exactly what Potiphar did, and it's exactly what the chief jailer
did. These powerful men all handed their power over to Joseph. And now,

Pharaoh himself, the Big Daddy of Power, the Nemesis of the Nile, is going to do the same thing. He just doesn't know it yet.

Joseph had been in the dungeon—Scripture calls it "the pit"—for two long years. As we have said, he may have thought he would live out his days in that dark, confining place. But suddenly, everything changed. Scripture says "they quickly brought him out of the pit" and "he came in before Pharaoh." Talk about going from one extreme to another! One minute in the pit, the next in the palace. One minute in the slammer, and the next minute standing before the most powerful man in the world.

That's the way it is sometimes in our walk with God. We feel hemmed in or trapped in some dark circumstance, and we pray and pray—until we begin to think that God lost our file somewhere. And then suddenly, at the precise right time, our sovereign King swings the door wide open and we're out of there, blinking in the bright morning light and savoring the fresh air. The waiting may seem endless to us, but God knows precisely where we are and how He intends to deliver us and restore us.

> And Pharaoh said to Joseph, "I have had a dream, and there is no one who can interpret it. I have heard it said of you that when you hear a dream you can interpret it." Joseph answered Pharaoh, "It is not in me; God will give Pharaoh a favorable answer." Then Pharaoh said to Joseph, "Behold, in my dream I was standing on the banks of the Nile. Seven cows, plump and attractive, came up out of the Nile and fed in the reed grass. Seven other cows came up after them, poor and very ugly and thin, such as I had never seen in all the land of Egypt. And the thin, ugly cows ate up the first seven plump cows, but when they had eaten them no one would have known that they had eaten them, for they were still as ugly as at the beginning. Then I awoke. I also saw in my dream seven ears growing on one stalk, full and good. Seven ears, withered,

thin, and blighted by the east wind, sprouted after them, and the thin ears swallowed up the seven good ears. And I told it to the magicians, but there was no one who could explain it to me." (vv. 15–24)

So here was the most feared king in the world looking to a young foreign slave to give him answers. So who was really in control of that situation? The answer is that Joseph was in control, because God had been preparing him throughout his entire life for this precise moment. God would give him the interpretation to the dream that God had commanded Pharaoh to dream.

If you freeze this picture of Joseph standing before Pharaoh, it drips with irony. The entire situation was orchestrated by God. Pharaoh is not in control of this situation. God is in control. And before it's all over, Pharaoh will do exactly what God wants him to do. Joseph will give Pharaoh a plan to prepare for the crisis. The plan was God's plan, and Pharaoh is going to follow it to the letter. And why will he do that? Because God is in control of powerful people.

## Another Powerful King

Sometimes it looks like powerful people are in *absolute* control with seemingly unlimited power.

Years ago, I had a lunch with a business executive who was in a state of shock. He had been with a very famous company for years, and this company had a policy of never laying off an employee. But along with thousands of others, he had been laid off due to a severe downturn in the company's financial health. It had been his plan to stay with the company for another six or seven years, and then he would be financially set for the rest of his life. After that, he had plans for the next twenty years of his life.

Now it was all in the Dumpster.

Understandably, this former executive had deep concerns about his future. His world had been turned upside down by the human-resources committee that decided to lay him off. He expressed his fear and anxiety about his future throughout the meal, and at one point I said to him, "You realize, don't you, that it was the Lord Jesus Christ who laid you off."

He looked at me like I had eaten too many MoonPies.

"What do you mean that the Lord laid me off? That committee laid me off!"

And then I said to him, "Do you really believe that the destiny of your life is in the hands of some committee? It was your plan to be there for seven more years, but it wasn't the Lord's plan. If *He* wanted you onboard for seven more years, that's right where you would have stayed. And no committee on earth could change that. The committee's heart is like channels of water in the hands of the Lord, and He turns it whatever way He wishes. He runs that committee, and He was the One who made them give you the boot. He's got something for you to do that wasn't in your plan—but it certainly is in His."

Now that's the way to look at the powerful people in your life. They have limited power given to them by God. And when He says jump, they jump—even if they don't believe in Him and even if they don't think He is great.

Remember my friend who was thrown into prison by the powerful judge? I got a letter from him last week. I think before his imprisonment he would have described himself as a Christian who had lost his spiritual priorities and was drifting from what he knew to be true. In the body of his letter, he wrote these words (and I quote with his permission):

> *Steve, I've had so much time to reflect, review and analyze my life it's been wonderful. I've never had so much alone time with just me and God. I have to be honest, doing a complete inventory of your life in front of God (and being brutally honest with yourself) is not an easy task. A lot of what I have found (or He has shown me), I didn't like. Now, it's up to me to do something about it. It seems like I have such clarity with His direction when I am*

*not being inundated with worldly issues. That is the one good thing about prison. You don't have any of those pressures. I am having to turn over every aspect of my life to God. What is funny or ironic about it is that while I sit here in prison, incarcerated physically, I have never been so spiritually free. I hope I explained that right. Paul does a much better job of writing from prison than I do.*

*God is talking to me all the time. I've really strayed over the past few years. It's amazing to me to feel His presence all the time. He promised to never leave me or forsake me.... It's a humbling and comforting feeling all in one.*

And then in the next paragraph, he asks a question.

*Steve, does God ever purposefully do "bad" things to His people to get them back into the fold?*

Bad things like having powerful judges break a plea agreement?
I wrote him back and said, "Yes."
And he agreed.
What a great God.

Chapter Nine

# He Programs the Weather Channel

## He Is in Control ...
## Over Famine, Weather, and Disasters

*"God had nothing to do with the events of September 11, 2001."*
*—anonymous pastor speaking on Christian television*

I n God We Trust" is imprinted on every coin issued in the United States. In 1588 England, the queen ordered that a gold medal be struck with the motto "He blew and they were scattered."[1]

*He blew and they were scattered?*

Why in the world would that phrase be put on a gold medal?

In May 1588, Spain was the most powerful nation on earth. And riding the crest of that power, the Spanish had set their sights on invading and capturing England. To accomplish that task, King Philip of Spain sent his navy—the most powerful navy on the seas. This fleet, made up of over a hundred warships, was known as the Invincible Armada. No nation on earth could hope to defeat it.

Departing Spain, the fleet sailed north toward England. Before they could attack, however, they ran into a monster storm—actually, a massive hurricane far north of the path hurricanes normally roam. And it was this staggering hurricane with its murderous winds that virtually annihilated the Spanish Armada.

This was the end of Spain as a world power.

The winds had stopped them before they could reach England. And all of England, including Queen Elizabeth, knew that God had sent the storm. "He blew and they were scattered" was the phrase of praise that was uttered in every village, pub, and church in all of England.

Not a word was said about "mother nature" or a chance event. All of the glory went to God the Father, God the Son, and God the Holy Spirit.


## Speaking of Disasters ...

This just came in from Fox News:

*An unnamed high official in Pharaoh's cabinet has confirmed the following information. God is going to open the gates and flood the economy with prosperity for the next seven years. And then ... He is going to turn off the tap and send a natural disaster that will plague Egypt and the surrounding nations for the following seven years.*

*That's what's coming, and it cannot be stopped.*

That was basically Joseph's answer to Pharaoh concerning the dreams that had so deeply disturbed the king. That good news would make the Egyptian stockbrokers and economists very happy. Inflation will be on its way down and earnings hitting the ceiling!

But what about the second part of that news bulletin—the part about God sending a long-term calamity that would threaten Egypt's very national existence?

Everyone in the palace probably had an opinion. And if it had been today, you could have heard the topic endlessly bandied about on talk radio. But there wasn't one thing Pharaoh or anyone else could do to keep it from happening.

> Then Joseph said to Pharaoh, "The dreams of Pharaoh are
> one; God has revealed to Pharaoh what he is about to do.

The seven good cows are seven years, and the seven good ears are seven years; the dreams are one. The seven lean and ugly cows that came up after them are seven years, and the seven empty ears blighted by the east wind are also seven years of famine. It is as I told Pharaoh; God has shown to Pharaoh what he is about to do. There will come seven years of great plenty throughout all the land of Egypt, but after them there will arise seven years of famine, and all the plenty will be forgotten in the land of Egypt. The famine will consume the land, and the plenty will be unknown in the land by reason of the famine that will follow, for it will be very severe. And the doubling of Pharaoh's dream means that the thing is fixed by God, and God will shortly bring it about. Now therefore let Pharaoh select a discerning and wise man, and set him over the land of Egypt. Let Pharaoh proceed to appoint overseers over the land and take one-fifth of the produce of the land of Egypt during the seven plentiful years. And let them gather all the food of these good years that are coming and store up grain under the authority of Pharaoh for food in the cities, and let them keep it. That food shall be a reserve for the land against the seven years of famine that are to occur in the land of Egypt, so that the land may not perish through the famine." (Gen. 41:25–36 ESV)

Dry and disastrous famines are bad news. People starve in famines. People die in famines. And God was sending one that would last for seven hard years.

Here's our problem. People die in tsunamis, earthquakes, and fires. And if God is in control of all of those events, then God is the One who made them die. If God is in control of those events, God is responsible for the physical and emotional wounds that result.

Fifty million people die every year, six thousand die every hour, and over one hundred people die every minute.[2] But when thousands of people die in the same place and at the same time, we are more likely to wonder why God would allow such a thing to happen.

Jerry Bridges offers his usual wise counsel:

> Many sensitive Christians struggle over the multitude of large-scale natural disasters around the world—an earthquake in one place, famine in another, typhoons and floods somewhere else. Thousands of people are killed, and others slowly starve to death. Entire regions are devastated, crops are ruined, homes destroyed. "Why does God allow all this?" we may ask. "Why does God permit all those innocent children to starve?"
>
> It is not wrong to wrestle with these issues, as long as we do it in a reverent and submissive attitude toward God. Indeed, to fail to wrestle with the issue of large-scale tragedy may indicate a lack of compassion toward others on our part. However, we must be careful not to, in our minds, take God off His throne of absolute sovereignty or put Him in the dock and bring Him to the bar of our judgment.[3]

## He's Still on the Throne

When a pastor says that God had nothing to do with the events of September 11 (as the quote at the beginning of this chapter indicates), he just took God off His throne. Now why is that pastor saying such a thing? I think he's trying to get God off the hook. He doesn't want God to come off looking like the bad guy. But by saying God had nothing to do with it, he digs an even deeper hole. If God had nothing to do with the events of September 11, then it somehow slipped through His system, and He isn't in absolute control.

The fact is, God doesn't need you to get Him off the hook. He doesn't need you to defend Him or explain Him. We may not know the purposes of God in sending the events of September 11, but that doesn't mean we deny that He was in control and even planned those events.

Because we love and honor God, we want everyone to feel good about Him and have all their questions answered. But that will never happen. Not for anyone. All of your questions and all of my questions about God will never be explained in this life. And if you are completely comfortable with the way that God works because you have weakened His power or diluted any of His other attributes in order to make Him more palatable for you, then you don't know the God of the Bible.

The God of the Bible is knowable, but He is also incomprehensible.

He does things that blow us away. *("My ways are not your ways.")*

At times He confuses us and other times He frustrates us. *("My thoughts are not your thoughts.")* At other times He pains us. And for reasons beyond our comprehension, He sometimes uses weather, terrorist attacks, and natural disasters to achieve His holy purposes.

His absolute power over nature astonishes us, as so described in Job 37:

> At this also my heart trembles
> and leaps out of its place.
> Keep listening to the thunder of his voice
> and the rumbling that comes from his mouth.
> Under the whole heaven he lets it go,
> and his lightning to the corners of the earth.
> After it his voice roars;
> he thunders with his majestic voice,
> and he does not restrain the lightnings when his voice is heard.
> God thunders wondrously with his voice;
> he does great things that we cannot comprehend.
> For to the snow he says, "Fall on the earth,"
> likewise to the downpour, his mighty downpour....

From its chamber comes the whirlwind,
and cold from the scattering winds.
By the breath of God ice is given,
and the broad waters are frozen fast.
He loads the thick cloud with moisture;
the clouds scatter his lightning.
They turn around and around by his guidance,
to accomplish all that he commands them
on the face of the habitable world.
Whether for correction or for his land
or for love, he causes it to happen.
(vv. 1–6, 9–13 ESV)

So when an earthquake kills thousands of people ... or a tsunami drowns tens of thousands ... or a hurricane levels a city ... or airliners are hijacked on 9/11 and thousands of people die ... what do we want?

We want to get God off the hook, don't we? We want to say that He had nothing to do with those things. But the Word of God says something entirely different:

If a calamity occurs in a city has not the LORD done it?
(Amos 3:6)

I am the LORD, and there is no other,
The One forming light and creating darkness,
Causing well-being and creating calamity;
I am the LORD who does all these.
(Isa. 45:6–7)

If you believe the Bible, there is no explaining away that God is in charge of calamity:

The term translated as "calamity" is the Hebrew word *ra* and is by far most often translated "evil" (also sometimes "bad," "harmful," or "wicked"). There is no stronger Hebrew word than this one for all that is ruinous and disastrous and wicked, both from the vantage point of human experience and as seen from God's own perspective.[4]

If there is any question that God claims to control calamities and disasters, note the following verses. Be warned—what these verses have to say may deeply disturb you.

> See now that I, even I, am he,
> and there is no god beside me;
> I kill and I make alive;
> I wound and I heal;
> and there is none that can deliver out of my hand.
> (Deut. 32:39 ESV)

> The LORD kills and brings to life;
> he brings down to Sheol and raises up.
> The LORD makes poor and makes rich;
> he brings low and He exalts.
> (1 Sam. 2:6–7 ESV)

> Who has spoken and it came to pass, unless the LORD has commanded it?
> Is it not from the mouth of the Most High that good and bad come?
> (Lam. 3:37–38 ESV)

## Not Easy Stuff

Dr. Bruce Ware carefully analyzes the teaching of these verses:

> Most Christians would affirm without hesitation that God
> has control over the good that happens; after all, James 1:17
> tells us that "every good gift" is from the Father of lights.
> So, it is not surprising or troubling to read in these passages
> that God makes alive, God heals, God raises up, God makes
> riches, God exalts, God brings about days of prosperity, God
> makes straight, God forms light, God makes well-being, and
> God brings about what is good. But what is amazing and
> instructive about these texts is that they attribute to God, in
> the same breath, human realities on the opposite side of the
> spectrum. Not only does God make alive, but God kills; not
> only does God heal, but God wounds. Indeed, God is said
> to make poor, to bring low, to make crooked, to bring about
> adversity, to create darkness, to create calamity, and to bring
> about what is bad....
>
> It is important that we simply allow the Scriptures to regis-
> ter in our thinking by letting these texts instruct us regarding
> the extent of God's sovereign control. Even if we cannot
> answer satisfactorily just *how* God controls good and evil
> without being morally compromised by his relation to evil,
> these texts affirm unambiguously *that* God so controls both.[5]

A few pages later in Dr. Ware's insightful book, he delves into the moral
implications of a God who controls both good *and* evil.

> God does reign over good and evil, over light and darkness,
> and with this biblical teaching as with many, many other

passages of Scripture, we concur that God controls everything that occurs in the created order. Everything!

Recall again that in Isaiah 45:7 God says, "I form light and create darkness." But alongside this passage, consider also 1 John 1:5: "This is the message we have heard from Him and proclaim to you, that God is Light, and in Him there is no darkness at all." How instructive! Although God controls *both light and darkness* (Isa. 45:7), God's own nature is exclusively *light and not darkness* (1 John 1:5).

> So while God controls well-being and calamity (evil), he does not delight in wickedness, nor does any evil dwell in him, nor can he even look upon evil (approvingly). In short, God is good and not evil though he controls both good and evil. His eternal and holy nature is in no way compromised. He is not stained by evil nor does he approve of evil. Evil is contrary to God's holy, moral nature, and his disposition toward evil is always one of hatred and opposition whereas his disposition toward good is always one of approval and embrace.[6]

We do not need to limit God and His power in order to resolve a moral dilemma concerning His responsibility for evil. We simply need to take the Scriptures for what they say.

## Hugging Trees, Hollowing Trees

I have a question: Does God need a permit to cut down a tree? The answer is no. God created trees and owns trees. He send His storms and fires, and trees are destroyed in the process.

But sometimes God chooses to just hollow out a tree.

Just recently a remarkable ceremony took place in Israel.

A survivor of the Nazi Holocaust touched a hollow tree trunk that he brought from Europe and told a spellbound audience in Israel: "It saved my life."

Polish-born Jakob Silberstein, presenting the tree to Jerusalem's Yad Vashem Holocaust Memorial, said he hid in its hollow trunk when German soldiers came looking for Jews in Czechoslovakia toward the end of World War II.

Silberstein, now eighty-three, found shelter during the war in the home of Jana Sudova, a Czech woman. Chasing a rabbit, he found the hollow tree in her yard and chose it as a possible hiding place should he be discovered.

As German troops were pulling out of the area, the Gestapo, the Nazi secret police, mounted one final search for Jews.

Silberstein bolted for the tree.

"It was so cramped in the tree. I was in there for nine hours and my heart was pounding, my whole body was trembling and I was sure that if the soldiers had come close to the tree they would have heard my breathing," he said.

"Towards the end I was so frightened but I didn't want to die in the tree. I feared that they might cut me up with a saw in the tree or shoot me," he added.

After the war, Silberstein settled in Israel. He returned to the Czech Republic in 2005; and with the help of a local journalist he managed to track down the tree, which had recently been cut down and was set to become garden furniture. He was given part of the trunk, which he then brought to Israel.

Silberstein's parents and three brothers were among some six million Jews whom Adolf Hitler's Nazi regime killed during World War II.[7]

God used a hollowed-out tree to save the life of a young boy. Did God plan for that tree to be hollowed out or did He just permit it? You may be thinking, *What does it matter?*

When it comes to hollow trees, it doesn't seem like an important question, but when it comes to evil, it's another matter entirely. Bruce Ware poses a question:

Is the notion of God "permitting" actions and events to occur a biblical idea? Consider these texts, where it seems clear that the biblical writers recognize and invoke this concept and way of speaking:

"Your father [Laban] has cheated me [Jacob] and changed my wages ten times. But *God did not permit him to harm me*" (Genesis 31:7).

… and they [the demons in the Gerasene demoniac] begged him, saying, "Send us to the pigs; let us enter them." *So he gave them permission.* And the unclean spirits came out, and entered the pigs (Mark 5:12–13).

"In past generations he allowed all the nations to walk in their own ways" (Acts 14:16).

"For I do not want to see you now just in passing. I hope to spend some time with you, *if the Lord permits*" (1 Corinthians 16:7).

"And this we will do *if the Lord permits*" (Hebrews 6:3).

Ware then provides the conclusion that helps us to solve the moral dilemma:

What needs to be understood here is that God is always able to permit only those occurrences of evil that he knows will serve his purposes and never thwart or hinder those purposes. He is able to do this because, for any evil that may occur, it is always in God's power to prevent that specific evil from happening.[8]

So the Lord permits evil to occur when it will serve His good and holy purposes. Do those occasions—which would include hurricanes, forest fires, mudslides, sickness, injury, and even death—always make sense to us?

No, they don't.

So we must be very careful of charging God with evil when He uses evil for His good purposes that we are not able to comprehend. It's a matter of trusting His goodness and His character when things just don't add up in our small minds.

## Back to Joseph

Joseph looked Pharaoh straight in the eye and said there were going to be seven very good years followed by seven years of absolute famine. Severe famine results from excruciating heat accompanied by prolonged drought. In other words, hot days and no rain. And when you plant your crops and get hot days and no rain for seven years, you've got a famine on your hands—a *major* natural disaster. Somebody call FEMA ... and hope that they show up!

The insurance companies call natural disasters "acts of God." Interesting, isn't it, that the insurance companies have more theological sense than some pastors today.

Can the same thing, then, be said of diseases that ravage our physical bodies?

My friend Paul Lanier is a medical doctor. His hobby is weight lifting. Paul attends my Wednesday-evening men's Bible study in Dallas and shows up just about every week.

But I should tell you something about Paul. Even though he is in his early forties, he doesn't practice medicine anymore. And he doesn't lift weights. As a matter of fact, Paul can no longer even lift his hand ... or walk into a room. When Paul comes into the study, his friends walk in with him, pushing his wheelchair.

Paul has Lou Gehrig's disease and has not been able to speak for several years. Most men who have this disease die within two to three years. Paul has had it for eight years. He has managed to survive so long probably due to the fact that he was in such extraordinary shape before the disease attacked his body.

The last thing I ever remember Paul saying to me before he lost his speech was remarkable. Paul said in very halting words, "Steve, this disease has saved my life. It has been a gift from God. It was this disease that brought me to Him. Without it, I would not have eternal life."

In Exodus 4:11 (NIV), we read this declaration of God's absolute control:

> Who gave man his mouth? Who makes him deaf or mute?
> Who gives him sight or makes him blind? Is it not I, the
> LORD?

Dr. Donald Grey Barnhouse, one of the great theologians and pastors of the previous century, comments on this straightforward text of Scripture:

> No person in this world was ever blind that God had not planned for him to be blind; no person was ever deaf in this world that God had not too planned for that person to be deaf…. If you do not believe that, you have a strange God who has a universe which has gone out of gear and He cannot control it.[9]

My friend Paul rejoices in the sovereignty of God. He's not bitter toward God for taking away his physical health. Does he like his circumstances? Of course not. But he knows that God is in control of his circumstances. He's trusting in the Lord to take care of his family after he is promoted to heaven. He knows that death is coming and that God has already planned the precise moment of his passing (Heb. 9:27). He is at peace with his future because he knows that God has planned his future. Paul doesn't serve a God who is confused about what will transpire in the future. He serves a God who *owns* the future, and everything in it—including tornadoes, earthquakes, cancer … and fog.

It was fog that saved nine thousand American soldiers under the command of George Washington on Friday, April 30, 1776. Trapped in Brooklyn, New York, the soldiers were sitting ducks for the shells of the British navy ships—and were on the verge of being surrounded by British troops. So Washington ordered a radical solution. They would evacuate all nine thousand men and their equipment, including wagons, by boat. They would have to make a mile-wide river crossing in the dark of night without any lights.

As soon as night fell, the soldiers began to load into the boats. Not a word was spoken aloud and not a light was lit. Throughout the night, crossing after crossing was made. With dawn soon approaching, however, many men remained to be evacuated. But astonishingly, just before the rays of dawn brought light to the scene, a heavy, thick fog descended. It was impossible to see more than six feet. "Even with the sun up, the fog remained as dense as ever, while over on the New York side of the river there was no fog at all."[10]

A little past seven in the morning, the last soldiers landed on the New York side of the river, and within minutes the thick fog lifted. Nine thousand American troops had been evacuated from the grasp of the enemy—with the aid of darkness and fog. As the fog lifted, the British officers were utterly astonished. They could see Washington's soldiers waving at them from the New York side.

In his book *1776*, David McCullough writes, "Incredibly, yet again, circumstances—fate, luck, Providence, the hand of God, as would be said so often—intervened."[11]

It wasn't fate.

It wasn't luck.

The same God who two hundred years earlier had saved the British navy, now confounded the British navy.

In 1588, "God blew and they were scattered."

In 1776, "God blew and the fog gathered."

David put it like this:

Our God is in the heavens;

He does whatever He pleases.

(Ps. 115:3)

## Ten Acts of God

The pages of Scripture are filled with accounts of divine intervention through the so-called forces of nature.

Some four hundred years after Joseph, Moses would stand before another pharaoh and tell him to let the people of Israel go from the land of Egypt. Pharaoh refused to obey, time and time again. So the Lord sent ten plagues upon Egypt. The ten plagues today would be known as natural disasters. Actually, they were supernatural disasters, or in other words, acts of God.

The water of the Nile was turned to blood (Ex. 7:14–25).

Frogs covered the land (Ex. 8:1–5).

Lice and/or gnats crawled everywhere in the land (Ex. 8:16–32).

Swarms of flies descended (Ex. 8:20–32).

The livestock of Egypt died overnight from disease (Ex. 9:1–7).

Painful boils broke out on man and beast (Ex. 9:8–12).

Destructive hail flattened the nation's crops (Ex. 9:13–35).

Swarms of locusts devoured everything green (Ex. 10:1–20).

Three days of thick darkness blanketed Egypt (Ex. 10:21–29).

Every firstborn in the land of Egypt died (Ex. 11:1—12:30).

The Egyptians and the children of Israel didn't live in the same town. The Jews lived in Goshen, but Goshen was right next door to the Egyptians. There was a border, and God acknowledged that border when He sent the plagues of nature (Ex. 8:22). The last seven plagues did not touch the Jews.

"Only the great God of Israel could control the flight pattern of tiny flies and keep them from entering the land of Goshen. But God's providential care of Israel was evident in all these seven last plagues, because the Jews escaped each one of them."[12]

This was an amazing demonstration of the power of God. Think of the plague of darkness. It was so dark in Egypt that the darkness could be *felt* (Ex. 10:21). Over in Goshen, however, the sun was shining warm and bright. The distinction was so clear that you could stand at the border on the Goshen side with the sun beaming down on your face and extend your hand over the border into Egypt and not see it because of the darkness.

The last plague was the worst. The firstborn of the Egyptians' children all perished in a night, as did the firstborn of all their livestock. But because each Jewish family sacrificed a lamb and put the blood of the lamb over the doorpost of the home, the angel of death passed over and the Hebrew firstborn lived.

What a wail of grief was heard throughout Egypt on that terrible night! Even Pharaoh's firstborn son was killed. It didn't have to happen. Pharaoh had been warned and told before each plague what God would do. If he would let the people of Israel go, no plague would come. But Pharaoh refused to obey. Each time he hardened his own heart. Ultimately, then, it was his fault that his son was dead along with all the other children in Egypt. He refused to bow the knee to the sovereign God of Israel and obey His will.

## The Greatest Pain

There is nothing deeper and darker than the death of a child. I am often asked by people when I teach on the providence of God about what one should say to grieving parents.

I want to walk very carefully here. I have never buried a child. I have never experienced that pain that is the deepest of all pains. So I don't know what that feels like. Joe Bayly did know what it felt like because he buried three of his sons. So I think we should hear what Joe said about speaking to grieving parents:

I was sitting, torn by grief. Someone came and talked to me of God's dealings, of why it happened, of why my loved one had died, of hope beyond the grave. He talked constantly. He said things I knew were true. I was unmoved, except to wish he'd go away. He finally did.

Another came and sat beside me. He didn't talk. He didn't ask me leading questions. He just sat beside me for an hour and more, listening when I said something, answered briefly, prayed simply, left. I was moved. I was comforted. I hated to see him go.

Joe Bayly offers great wisdom from his personal pain. Joe was a pastor and a theologian. He knew that God is sovereign and absolutely in control. He knew full well the grief of Job, and he knew that the Lord gives and the Lord takes away. But what he needed in his pain was not verses; he needed a listening friend who was willing to sit beside him and say nothing.

Joe is now in heaven with his three sons who preceded him, enjoying the presence of Jesus Christ. They have no pain and no sorrow. But it was not that way on earth. God is sovereign in heaven and on the earth. But when earthly sons and daughters die young, it is excruciatingly painful.

We must be very careful indeed what we say to grieving parents. To simply say to them that "God is in control" will provide little comfort, even though deep-down they know it to be the truth. May God give us wisdom in such situations.

Sometimes children die. Others suffer with lingering disease. And the only source of comfort in the entire universe is the truth that there is a sovereign God who is good and does good (Ps. 119:68)—even when evil strikes.

Margaret Clarkson says it so well:

The sovereignty of God is the one impregnable rock to which the suffering human heart must cling. The circumstances surrounding our lives are no accident; they may be the work of evil, but that evil is held firmly within the mighty hand of our sovereign God…. All evil is subject to Him, and evil cannot touch His children unless He permits it. God is the Lord of human history and of the personal history of every member of His redeemed family.[13]

# Back to 9/11

This chapter began with a small quote under the chapter title from a pastor concerning the events of September 11, 2001. The pastor said, "God had nothing to do with the events of September 11, 2001."

We often ask why so many suffered and died on that dreadful day in our nation's history. But what we should be asking is how many were brought to Christ through the devastation of September 11.

Is it not possible that the Lord used Hurricane Katrina to bring many into the kingdom?

He used a broken father like Joe Bayly to proclaim the gospel at the funeral of his eldest son—and numerous young men and women came to Christ.

Joe Bayly would have preferred for God to have used another method.

And so would Paul Lanier.

But they also knew this: His ways are not our ways. But His ways are always right and good—even when they are beyond our ability to comprehend.

Chapter Ten

# Climbing the Egyptian Ladder

## He Is in Control ...
## Over All Promotion and Advancement

*"I want it all and I want it now."*
—*rock band Queen*

A slave at seventeen and a king at thirty.

That was Joseph's story. It is the greatest promotion in history, and he didn't have to embellish his résumé to get it.

According to a recent study, over 50 percent of Americans have lied on their résumés. "A 2004 report by the Government Accountability Office found that 463 government employees in eight federal agencies listed bogus academic credentials on their résumés. Twenty-eight of the fibbers held senior-level positions, a number the GAO called 'an understatement.'"[1] The most senior fakers included three managers with top security clearance at the National Nuclear Security Administration and executives at the Departments of Homeland Security and Transportation. They obviously agree with the advice of W. C. Fields: "Anything worth winning is worth cheating for."

But if you serve a God who is in control of everything, including promotion, then you don't need to falsify your résumé to make yourself look better.

Instead of saying that you graduated from college when you actually didn't, just put on your résumé that you were really stupid and dropped out just six classes short of graduating. Go ahead—put it down. They'll appreciate your honesty. And the Lord takes care of those who are honest enough to tell the truth. He is big enough to take care of your promotions without your lying about your achievements. If the Lord could handle Joseph's career, He can certainly handle yours.

After thirteen years of continuous storms, turbulence, upheaval, and disappointment, it was finally over. In less than an hour, Joseph went from the pit to the pinnacle, from a dungeon to actually co-ruling with the most powerful man on the face of the earth.

Joseph went from the lowest place in Egypt to the highest office in the land in less time than it takes to get kids ready for school.

It was a stunning promotion.

Pharaoh knew a first-round draft choice when he saw one. Joseph laid out the urgency and the plan in a very convincing manner:

> "The doubling of Pharaoh's dream means that the thing is fixed by God, and God will shortly bring it about. Now therefore let Pharaoh select a discerning and wise man, and set him over the land of Egypt. Let Pharaoh proceed to appoint overseers over the land and take one-fifth of the produce of the land of Egypt during the seven plentiful years. And let them gather all the food of these good years that are coming and store up grain under the authority of Pharaoh for food in the cities, and let them keep it. That food shall be a reserve for the land against the seven years of famine that are to occur in the land of Egypt, so that the land may not perish through the famine."
>
> This proposal pleased Pharaoh and all his servants. And Pharaoh said to his servants, "Can we find a man like this, in whom is the Spirit of God?" Then Pharaoh said to Joseph, "Since

God has shown you all this, there is none so discerning and wise as you are. You shall be over my house, and all my people shall order themselves as you command. Only as regards the throne will I be greater than you." And Pharaoh said to Joseph, "See, I have set you over all the land of Egypt." Then Pharaoh took his signet ring from his hand and put it on Joseph's hand, and clothed him in garments of fine linen and put a gold chain about his neck. And he made him ride in his second chariot. And they called out before him, "Bow the knee!" Thus he set him over all the land of Egypt. Moreover, Pharaoh said to Joseph, "I am Pharaoh, and without your consent no one shall lift up hand or foot in all the land of Egypt." (Gen. 41:32–44 ESV)

Before Joseph knew what was happening, the thirteen-year-old storm was over. The clouds rolled back, and brilliant sunshine flooded the landscape of his life. Nothing would ever be the same.

Who knows? God may do something like that for you. And if you think that is highly unlikely, you are precisely the kind of person He loves to shock with His boundless goodness and grace.

It was Thomas Watson who observed that "God works strangely. He brings order out of confusion, harmony out of discord. He frequently makes use of unjust men to do that which is just."[2]

That is precisely what happened when Joseph was promoted. It may have been the strangest and most unlikely promotion in all of history.

## A Question in Heaven

I have something I want to ask Joseph when I see him in heaven. I want to ask him how he was doing that morning before he was summoned to see Pharaoh. I want to know if he got up looking forward to the day as he put on the coffee.

I want to know if he was singing as he was in the shower. I want to ask Joseph how he was doing on a scale of 1 to 10, with 10 being the top. How was he doing emotionally?

Can I tell you what I suspect? I don't think Joseph was doing real well. I don't think he was walking around the house singing, "This is the day that the Lord has made, I will rejoice and be glad in it."

I can't prove it and I have no specific evidence from Scripture to support my theory. The only biblical support I can offer to my theory is that Joseph was about to be resurrected.

And last time I checked, before you can have a resurrection, you've got to have a death.

I'm thinking to myself that Joseph wasn't doing well because he had endured this life-storm for thirteen years, with the last two in Pharaoh's dungeon. He had been in the prison for two years. During that two-year stint, he had not heard a single word from the cupbearer.

I can tell you this: If I were Joseph and I had been in that situation for thirteen years with absolutely no prospects of ever seeing my circumstances change, my personal hopes and dreams would be verging on death.

And that was the moment he was summoned to appear before Pharaoh.

## The Truth about Promotion

As I look at the story of Joseph and marvel at the providence of God in his promotion and advancement, several clear principles jump out at me. Joseph's promotion was the culmination of a long and difficult thirteen-year stretch of disappointment and turmoil. But all of this, including Joseph's remarkable promotion, was linked together by the providence of God.

At the end of Joseph's storm, there was a

*prompt promotion*, as a result of his being

*properly positioned* by God after a long season of

*patient preparation,* which included a significant test where Joseph was
*purposely purified.*

The prompt promotion took place after years and years of frustration and waiting. At times Joseph must have thought things would never change. But in God's timing, they changed in a way that he never could have imagined. Ephesians 3:20 (NKJV) declares, "Now to Him who is able to do exceedingly abundantly above all that we ask or think, according to the power that works in us." I'm sure Joseph had a vivid imagination. But never in his wildest dreams could he have conjured up what God had planned for him.

Bear in mind, however, that he didn't *start* at the top. He went through a process. And as we saw in an earlier chapter, before God promotes, He tests. Before God could hand Joseph such a massive amount of power and responsibility, he had to be tested in the area of his purity.

## Purposefully Purified

As a young man, Joseph was undoubtedly very gifted. His quick climb through the levels of promotion in Potiphar's household—until he was running the entire operation—revealed him to be a quick study. He must have had excellent people skills and high intelligence. But we have all seen gifted young people with tremendous potential who were lacking one key element: character.

Joseph's character was tested daily by Potiphar's wife as she tried to seduce Joseph without success. Joseph knew he was accountable to God for his actions and behavior. But the relentless woman would not quit. Joseph was a young man who was enormously talented. But God made sure that he was purposefully purified as he daily endured the fire of sexual temptation that came from Potiphar's wife.

I was reminded recently of how critically essential purity is in the lives of those who would desire to be used by God. I'm thinking of a phone call with a guy I hadn't talked to in close to fifteen years. He had just turned forty. I knew him when he was just married and in his twenties.

This man is nothing short of brilliant. If I'm not mistaken, he got a perfect score on the SAT. When I met him, he had just finished his first doctorate at the age of twenty-three. When I talked with him last week, he told me that he now has three earned doctorates. He was raised in a strong Christian home. His grandfather was a pastor. This guy probably knows the words of every hymn ever written in the history of Christianity. Throughout his life, he remained involved in church up to his eyeballs, faithfully attending services every Sunday and his small group during the week.

Back when I met him, he was newly married and just launching his career. Wealthy and successful in business, my young friend gave generously to the work of the Lord. I remember him calling me and asking me about a specific ministry he was interested in. I found out later he wrote a check for over $25,000 to that ministry—and he wasn't even twenty-five yet.

He called one day to have lunch with me because he wanted to talk with me about sexual temptation. He had read my book *Point Man*, and he asked, "Why are the first hundred pages of that book about sexual temptation?"

"Because," I replied, "I think that's the biggest temptation that men face."

"Do you really think it's that big of a problem?" he asked.

"I honestly do," I replied.

For the next hour he asked me question after question about sexual temptation. He really didn't see it as that big of an issue. What I didn't know was that this newly married guy had already gotten another woman pregnant. He hadn't been married a year and already he was living a lie.

I thought that he was looking for biblical guidance. He wasn't. He knew the truth already. He knew what the Scriptures said. But this guy was fighting the wisdom of the Great Guide of heaven. He knew the direction that God wanted him to take, he just didn't want to do it. He really wasn't interested in passing the purity/character test.

What he was trying to do was to figure out how he could get around it and still be viewed as a spiritual man.

This man still makes great money. But behind him there is one train wreck after another. Every time he faces a critical decision, he reads his Bible and then decides to go the wrong way. He has left behind him a trail of broken wives and broken children. And he's only forty. How many more lives will he ruin before he's done?

This guy is so smart that he's stupid.

He can ace the SAT, but he has no interest in passing the purity test. And in spite of his incredible giftedness and potential, God will never use him.

And that is his choice. He wouldn't have resisted Potiphar's wife for five minutes. The fact is, he wouldn't want to resist her. So by this choice he has decided the course of his life.

Thank God that Joseph took a different course.

## Patiently Prepared

Throughout the pages of this book, we have examined the process of preparation through which God took Joseph. Thirteen years is a long, long time. But when you consider the fact that Joseph would become the co-ruler of Egypt at the age of thirty, and that he wouldn't die until he was one hundred ten years old, thirteen years really wasn't all that much time in the big picture.

When God wants to do a great work in our lives, He will take the time necessary to develop the internal traits in our lives that are necessary for the task ahead of us.

William Wilberforce was a young man who was wasting his life. But God had something in mind for him. He was going to use him to eradicate slavery from the British Empire.

As a college student, Wilberforce was living off his trust fund, partying hard, and thinking about no one other than himself. He had a marvelous mind and was extremely articulate and persuasive. But those gifts were ignored and neglected as William continued to drink and spend money on his friends and the pursuit of pleasure. That was pretty much his life: friends and fun.

William liked to drink and he liked to play cards—for money. He didn't cheat when he gambled, but he had such a great mind that he was miles ahead of the other players. He was at his best playing for high stakes. He was making more playing cards than most grown men would make at a responsible job. He was enrolled in college but was rapidly wasting the opportunity. He would rather stay up late and hang out with his friends than get up early and go to class.

It was time for him to decide what he was going to do with his life. As a member of the wealthy upper class in England in the late 1700s, William decided that he should go into politics. He ran for office and spent $320,000 to win. He was now a young, wealthy, and privileged member of Parliament. But he had no sense of purpose or direction. In his later writings, he admitted that he wasted his first three to four years in Parliament.

A profound change took place in his life between the winter of 1784, when he was twenty-five, and the late summer of 1785. He began to spend time with his former schoolmaster, Isaac Milner. To the shock of Wilberforce, he discovered that Milner had become a committed follower of Christ.

Over the next year, his objections and intellectual doubts began to erode away, one by one. He found himself moving from "intellectual assent" to "profound conviction."[3] When he confessed with his mouth Jesus as Lord, and believed in his heart that God raised Him from the dead (Rom. 10:9–10), Wilberforce became a new creature in Christ. He referred to his conversion experience as "the great change."[4]

God patiently prepared Wilberforce just as He did Joseph. In reading the Englishman's biography, it became clear to me that he, too, walked through a series of testings that would determine his character and absolute allegiance to Christ. He knew heartbreak and disappointments. They would be with him for the rest of his life. But all the time, the providence of God was sustaining him through the storms that continually came into his life.

We look back in history and marvel at the way God used Wilberforce. The lives of hundreds of thousands of people, down through the generations, were positively influenced by the life of this man. He not only freed the slaves of the British Empire, but he used his wealth to set up Christian schools and orphanages throughout England. He was a man who touched the lives of others everywhere he went.

But God had to take him through years of difficulty and personal brokenness to prepare him for the work that lay ahead of him.

At times he would become weary. Does that sound familiar to you? Do you ever get weary—fatigued by wave after wave of hardship and trial? Wilberforce knew these waves in the storm and so did Joseph.

These men were not exempt from personal hardship.

Neither are you.

But these hardships and afflictions come straight from the hand of an infinitely loving heavenly Father—and they are designed to deepen us and strengthen us and give us the endurance we need for the work that lies ahead of us. Anyone who has ever been used by God has gone through this process.

There are no shortcuts.

But God will sustain you and make a way for you through the difficulties.

Martyn Lloyd-Jones made the following observation. It has been a great source of encouragement to me over the years:

> Faith says, What He has begun to do He can continue to do. The beginning of the work was a miracle, so if He can initiate a miraculous work He can keep it going; what He has already begun He can continue. "Being confident," Paul says, "of this very thing, that He who began a good work in you will bring it to completion until the day of Christ Jesus" (Phil. 1:6).
>
> Yes, says (the poet), Toplady,

"The work which His goodness began
The arm of His strength will complete."
That is an unanswerable argument.[5]

It's an unanswerable argument because if God starts a good work, God will sustain the work and finish the work. That's what He did with Joseph and with William Wilberforce, and He's doing the same in your life. He's not interested in doing a superficial work. He wants to do a *deep* work.

F. B. Meyer offers us some great insight when he writes,

> Psalm 105:18, referring to Joseph's imprisonment, has a striking alternative reading, "His soul entered into iron." Turning that around, and rendering it in our language, it reads thus, *Iron entered into his soul.* Is there not a truth in this? It may not be the truth intended in that verse, but it is a very profound truth: Sorrow and deprivation, the yoke borne in the youth, and the soul's enforced restraint are all conducive to an iron tenacity and strength of purpose, an endurance, a fortitude, that are the indispensable foundation and framework of a noble character. Do not flinch from suffering. Bear it silently, patiently, resignedly. Be assured that it is God's way of infusing iron into your spirituality.[6]

## Properly Positioned

As part of His providential plan for Joseph's life, God continually placed Joseph in the right place at the right time. That's why Joseph was in precisely the right position for the promotion God had in mind to give him.

The place of His providential positioning was a jail.

Isn't that just like the Lord?

He is so infinitely creative in His providence. God can use a jail, a wheelchair, a divorce, a career setback, or a loss of reputation to providentially and properly position us for the work that He has for us to do.

It's absurd to think that a foreign slave in an Egyptian jail would sixty minutes later be sharing power with the most powerful man on the face of the earth. But that's precisely what happened in God's sovereign plan.

*Your current position is not a problem to God and His plans for your life.* As a matter of fact, He is the One who positions us in the first place.

Let's go back to William Wilberforce for a minute. He wasn't in jail; he was in Parliament. But as the Lord began to work in his life, he wanted to maximize his life for the Lord. At the age of twenty-six, he began to completely refocus his direction. He had wasted several good years, and he wanted to get back on track. He pondered leaving politics and going into ministry. But a wise pastor by the name of John Newton (the man who penned the hymn "Amazing Grace") urged him to use his gifts in politics and stay in Parliament. God could use men in politics just as He could use men at a pulpit.

Wilberforce had a hard time with that. He thought he needed to go into full-time ministry to really be used by God. But the wise old pastor finally convinced him that he was already in a providential position.

With that counsel, the purpose of his life started to become clear.

"More than a year after his spiritual transformation, on Sunday, October 28, 1787, he found his life's work. On a blank page in his diary, 'God Almighty has set before me two great objects, the suppression of the slave trade and the reformation of morals.' From that time forward, he would pursue these objects with a determination unprecedented in the history of his country."[7]

William Wilberforce decided to get on the right path and make something of his life. And he did. He was the man who stood up against slavery and led the battle to bring it to a halt across the vast British Empire. It took him twenty years to wipe out Britain's slave trade, and another twenty-six to abolish slavery altogether in British colonies and elsewhere.[8]

He was called the George Washington of humanity. And no less of a leader than Abraham Lincoln honored his example and character. Charles

Colson observes, "Had William Wilberforce remained content with life that Providence had given him, he might easily have become prime minister of Great Britain and, consequently, the most powerful political leader of his day. He was wealthy, well-educated, witty, a fine singer and a brilliant speaker, with no peers at having fun or attracting a crowd … but his life, in one pivotal moment, took a very different turn. For God, it seems, had other plans for William Wilberforce."[9]

Did things easily fall into place for Wilberforce as he sought God's purpose and work for his life? The answer is no. Every day was a struggle and a fight. His battle against slavery consumed forty-six years of his life (from 1787 to 1833).[10]

> The defeats and setbacks along the way would have caused the ordinary politician to embrace a more popular cause. Though he never lost a parliamentary election from age twenty-one to seventy-four, the cause of abolishing the slave trade was defeated eleven times before its passage in 1807. And the battle for abolishing slavery itself did not gain the decisive victory until three days before he died in 1833.[11]

Wilberforce was promoted by God and then went about his work of abolishing slavery in the British Empire. When the work was done, he died three days later. But until his work was done, he couldn't die.

## Promptly Promoted

When God decides to promote, it's a done deal. No one can stay His hand or frustrate His plan. One morning Joseph was supervising the jail—the next he was riding in Pharaoh's chariot as people bowed before him.

Psalm 75:6–7 (AB) clearly states that promotion is from the Lord:

For not from the east nor from the west nor from the south
come promotion and lifting up.
>    But God is the Judge! He puts down one and lifts up another.

But as we have seen, before the promotion comes, God tests us and strengthens us through hardship and trials.

## Parallels Between Joseph and Jesus

The story of Joseph is breathtaking in its exhaustive evidence of the sovereignty and providence of God that He works in the lives of His people. But it has been noted by many that the life of Joseph foreshadows the coming and work of the Lord Jesus Christ.

- Joseph was rejected by his brethren; Jesus by the Jews, His brethren according to the flesh.
- Joseph was sold for twenty pieces of silver to Ishmaelites; Jesus was sold by the treachery of Judas for thirty pieces.
- Joseph was cast into prison; Jesus was put into the tomb.
- Joseph in prison preached deliverance to the cupbearer; Jesus went and proclaimed the gospel to the spirits in prison.
- Joseph had two fellow prisoners, one was delivered and one died; Jesus had two criminals with Him at Calvary, one who was forgiven and the other who chose eternal death.
- Joseph was promoted to the throne; Jesus is at the Father's right side of the throne, and will soon come as King of Kings and Lord of Lords.[12]

Some would look at all of that and call it sheer coincidence.
But by now, we know it is nothing less than divine providence.

## Chapter Eleven

# From Womb to Tomb

## He Is in Control …
## Over Every Event of Your Life,
## and Will Work It for Good

*"Did you never run for shelter in a storm,*
*and find fruit which you expected not?*
*Did you never go to God for safeguard,*
*driven by outward storms,*
*and there find unexpected fruit?"*
—*John Owen*

When they started their voyage in 1831, the two men had much in common.

Both voyagers were Christians and believed that a sovereign God had created the world, just as Genesis records. Their journey on the HMS *Beagle* would take five years to complete. When they returned to England, however, only one of the men, Captain Robert FitzRoy, considered himself a follower of Christ and a believer in His Word. Charles Darwin had abandoned his faith and was about to publish his writings on his theory of evolution.

FitzRoy was a brilliant navigator and the inventor of the FitzRoy barometer. He had a productive and significant career and served as governor of New

Zealand. But he was haunted for the rest of his life that he had been the one who had captained the ship that became the setting for Darwin's radical teaching. If he had known what Darwin would ultimately publish, he never would have taken him onboard. FitzRoy felt somehow responsible for the great heresy of evolution that had led so many away from God and the truth of the Scriptures. The evil that Darwin had done while under his charge was blood on his hands—or so he thought.

Finally, in 1865, suffering under great emotional pain and staggering depression, he took his own life.

FitzRoy could never reconcile himself with the evil that Darwin had done. The focus of his entire life became the five-year journey on the HMS *Beagle*, which resulted in Darwin's theory of evolution. And because he could not get his eyes off the evil, it eventually destroyed him.

His eyes should have been on the God who intended it for good.

## A Perspective on Providence

Evil is real, and it has happened to all of us.

When Joseph addressed his brothers, he did not downplay or diminish what they had done to him. When they sold him into slavery at the age of seventeen, they intended it for evil (Gen. 50:20).

They *knew* they had done evil to him.

When their father died, the evil they had done was the source of their anxiety, worry, and guilt: "What if Joseph bears a grudge against us and pays us back in full for all the wrong which we did to him!" (Gen. 50:15).

Fully aware of what they were doing, they had conspired and planned an evil deed against their own flesh and blood.

Joseph Goebbels was Hitler's most trusted confidant. A brilliant man who was bitter over his club foot and his small stature, he became the minister of propaganda for Hitler, and an influential strategist who sold the Nazi lie to the German people.

Paul Johnson, an eminent historian, tells of a secret briefing that Goebbels gave to some select German journalists on April 5, 1940, just four days before the Nazi invasion of Norway. One of the journalists wrote a transcript, quoting Goebbels in the secret meeting. With his guard down, Goebbels talked freely of how Hitler rose to power:

> Up to now we have succeeded in leaving the enemy in the dark concerning Germany's real goals, just as before 1932 our domestic foes never saw where we were going or that our oath of legality was just a trick. We wanted to come to power legally, but we did not want to use power legally.... They could have suppressed us. They could have arrested a couple of us in 1925 and that would have been that, the end. No, they let us through the danger zone. That's exactly how it was in foreign policy too.... In 1933 the French premier ought to have said (and if I had been the French premier I would have said it): "The new Reich Chancellor is the man who wrote *Mein Kampf,* which says this and that. This man cannot be tolerated in our vicinity. Either he disappears or we march!" But they didn't do it. They left us alone and let us slip through the risky zone, and we were able to sail around all dangerous reefs. *And when we were done, and well armed, better than they, then they started the war.*[1]

As this evil group plotted their evil plan, so Joseph's brothers planned and plotted evil against him in order to remove him from their lives. And as a result, they were willing to do violence against him, and then lie to their father about Joseph's disappearance.

## Violence and Lying

Violence and lying are always a part of evil. And they always go hand in hand.

Alexander Solzhenitsyn, the Russian dissident who spoke out against the torture and mass murders of Stalin and his followers, spent many years in a Siberian prison camp. It was in that horrid Gulag that he found Christ. Years later, when he came to America, he was awarded the Nobel Peace Prize. But his straightforward speech met with much criticism. That should not be surprising since it contained so much truth. In his speech, he demonstrated the link between violence and lies:

> Let us not forget that violence does not and cannot flourish by itself; it is inevitably intertwined with lying. Between them there is the closest, the most profound and natural bond: nothing screens violence except lies, and the only way lies can hold is by violence.
>
> Whoever has once announced violence as his method must inevitably choose lies as his principle.... The simple act of an ordinary courageous man is not to take part, not to support lies! Let the lie come into the world, even dominate the world, but not through me.[2]

We all know that September 11, 2001, was the day that evil made a searing attack on our nation's affluent and prosperous way of life.

Os Guinness writes of that day:

> The date September 11, 2001, was marked down in my calendar for a dinner discussion in Manhattan—on the theme of evil. When the dinner did take place a week after the ruthless terrorist strike, the only other people in the hotel

were the survivors from an investment firm that had lost nearly seventy people in the tragedy. One of them, who attended our discussion, had made it down safely from the 104th floor of the second tower and was a harrowing witness to the day of terror. As our host said in introducing some of the key readings on evil, "When I read some of these readings before September 11, I thought they were far too dark. When I read them again after September 11, they weren't nearly dark enough."[3]

It's remarkable that our perspective about evil could change so rapidly.

## Personal Pain

We have all been the recipients of evil acts. Someone has plotted against you to hurt and harm you. It may be a coworker, an ex-spouse, or someone even in your own family. There are degrees to evil and degrees to our individual experiences with someone plotting evil against us. But no matter what the degree of evil, violence, or lies that come against you, one thing can be said that applies to all of us:

The greatest evil is to lose your own soul.

The greatest evil is to be without Christ.

But if you are in Christ, God is your Father. And that changes everything when it comes to the evil, violence, and lying that is sent against us.

*"You meant it for evil against me, but God intended it for good, in order to bring about this present result."*

There is nothing more astonishing about the providence of God than this: He is able to take the evil that comes against you and wounds you and those near to you, and He promises to work it out for good.

Joseph understood that truth, and it saved him from becoming a bitter man. Robert FitzRoy didn't have that perspective, and it drove him to suicide.

The apostle Paul put it in these familiar words: "And we know that God causes all things to work together for good to those who love God, to those who are called according to His purpose" (Rom. 8:28).

That verse doesn't say that all things are good. It acknowledges that kidnapping, rape, divorce, incest, adultery, violence, and other assorted symptoms of the human heart are *not* good. But what it does say is that God takes the evil things, the bad things, that come into our lives, and He *works them* for the good of those who love Him and have been called by Him.

This is exactly what Joseph declared to his brothers: The evil that you manufactured and brought against me to ruin my life—that very same evil God intended for good to bring about this present result. The present result was that Joseph was co-ruler of Egypt and able to provide for and comfort the ones who had actually planned to undo him. What a strange outcome of such complex events—but what a wonder of an outcome.

Thomas Watson writes,

> See here the wisdom of God, who can make the worst things imaginable turn to the good of the saints.... The Lord made Joseph's prison a step to preferment.... God enriches by impoverishing.... God works strangely. He brings order out of confusion, harmony out of discord.... God often helps when there is least hope, and saves his people in that way which they think will destroy.... God's ways are "past finding out" (Rom. 11:33). They are rather to be admired than fathomed. There is never a providence of God, but has either a mercy or a wonder in it.[4]

Joseph's entire life had become a wonder that reflected the goodness and the providence of God. God had taken the great evil calculated against him and turned it for his good. The birth of Joseph's two sons clearly displayed that perspective:

> Before the year of famine came, two sons were born to Joseph. Asenath, the daughter of Potiphera priest of On, bore them to him. Joseph called the name of the firstborn Manasseh. "For," he said, "God has made me forget all my hardship and all my father's house." The name of the second he called Ephraim, "For God has made me fruitful in the land of my affliction." (Gen. 41:50–52 ESV)

The comments of Warren Wiersbe on this passage are worth noting:

> The name Manasseh means "forgetting." Joseph didn't forget his family or the events that occurred, but he did forget the pain and suffering they caused. He realized that God meant it for good (50:20). Therefore, looking at the past from that perspective, he attained victory over his bad memories and bitterness.
>
> The name Ephraim means "twice fruitful." Egypt had been a place of affliction for Joseph, but now he had two sons and was fruitful in the land. But even more, he would become fruitful as the second ruler of the land and be used of God to save many lives, including his own family and the nation of Israel.[5]

They meant it for evil but God intended it for good. And those two boys were living testimonies to Joseph of the goodness of God. As Joseph watched his sons grow up, he must have marveled over God's faithfulness again and again. When he thought his life was over, it was just beginning. The hand of God had been upon Joseph his entire life, even when his future looked bleak and nonexistent. But as we have seen, "the LORD was with Joseph" (Gen. 39:2).

The Lord was with Joseph, and the Lord is with you.

For after all, we have the same Father. That's why He will turn the evil and work it for our good. As we have seen, He never makes a mistake or a misstep. Even when it makes no earthly sense to us, He is working for our good. And by now we realize that the best perspective for seeing this is to look backward. And when we do, as R. C. Sproul suggests, we can see His invisible hand. For if any one link in the chain of our lives was missing, it all would have gone a different direction:

> If we play the "what if" game with Joseph, we go back to the technicolored coat. If there had been no coat, perhaps there would not have been so much envy and jealousy among his brothers. No jealousy, no selling to the Midianite traders. And if the Midianite traders had been heading in the opposite direction, Joseph would have never have gone to Egypt. No Egypt, no selling to Potiphar. Had someone else purchased him, there would have been no encounter with Potiphar's wife. No Potiphar's wife, no prison. No prison, no meeting with the baker and the butler. No meeting with the butler, no meeting with Pharaoh to interpret his dream. No meeting with Pharaoh, and Joseph would never have become prime minister.
>
> If we telescope this collection of "what ifs?" we conclude that if it were not for Joseph's technicolored coat there would be no Christianity, and every chapter of human history would have a different ending.[6]

In other words, *HE IS IN CONTROL.*

I close this book with a prayer. It is a prayer that comes from John Rylands. Though the prayer was penned more than a hundred years ago, its message is as fresh and relevant as this morning's sunrise.

God be praised for His loving watch-care and control over our lives!

*Sovereign Ruler of the skies,*
*Ever gracious, ever wise,*
*All my times are in thy hand,*
*All events at thy command.*

*His decree who formed the earth*
*Fixed my first and second birth;*
*Parents, native place, and time,*
*All appointed were by him.*

*He that formed me in the womb,*
*He shall guide me to the tomb;*
*All my times shall ever be*
*Ordered by his wise decree.*

*Times of sickness; times of health;*
*Times of penury and wealth;*
*Times of trial and of grief;*
*Times of triumph and relief;*

*Times the tempter's power to prove;*
*Times to test the Savior's love,*
*All must come, and last, and end*
*As shall please my heavenly friend.*

*Plagues and death around me fly;*
*Till he bids, I cannot die.*
*Nor a single shaft can hit*
*Till the love of God sees fit.*[7]

# Study Questions for Personal Reflection or Small-Group Discussion

## Chapter 1: Strangely and Slowly, God Is Working

1. Hated and cruelly betrayed by his own brothers, Joseph certainly qualified for the title of victim. Yet somehow, through all the dizzying ups and downs of his life, he never seemed to wear that label. How was Joseph able to keep his head up and maintain trust in God through horrendous personal circumstances?

2. The author calls the sovereignty of God "a feisty capsule that tends to stick in our throats and cause us great discomfort." Has that been true for you? If so, what aspects of that sovereign control trouble you most?

3. John Flavel said, "Some providences of God, like Hebrew letters, are best understood backwards." In your own words, explain what this statement implies for your life. What can you see when you look "backwards"?

4. The providence of God speaks of His absolute control. How might that bring comfort when desperate and even evil circumstances crash into your life?

5. Joseph knew very well that his elevation to the office of prime minister of Egypt wasn't the result of chance, coincidence, fate, or dumb luck. In fact, he saw God's intentions written all over that miraculous promotion. (See Genesis 50:20.) How can acknowledging God's providence and sovereignty in the promotions of life give you that all-important perspective for the inevitable setbacks and even seeming disasters you may experience?

6. Imagine a universe where God was not sovereign and did not have full control. How would you feel about facing an uncertain future? What would concern you or make you feel insecure?

# Chapter 2: When Your Dreams Die

1. Dr. Warfield said that nothing that occurs in God's universe takes Him by surprise, nor can He be imagined to be indifferent to those happenings, though He "sees it coming." But why wouldn't we feel that God doesn't care when He allows tragedies in our lives that He could have easily prevented?

2. The author writes that when Joseph was in the midst of his life's worst storms, "it seemed like his life had spun completely out of control." Think of a time in your life when events seemed random and out of control. What did you think about God and His plan for your life during that time? Can you think of a way you might have found a better perspective?

3. Being betrayed by his own brothers had to have hurt Joseph like a two-by-four across the chops. How can we keep from being overwhelmed by negative emotions in such moments?

4. The author writes of Joseph, "If the providence of God hadn't shown up at the exact right moment, he would have died. If God had been just fifteen seconds late, it would have been too late to save him." Think back to an incident like that in your own life. How did the providence of God rescue you?

5. John Flavel says, "Learn to adore providence." When you recognize that providence, the author says, when something like that happens, "you don't write it off to coincidence. *You give glory to God.*" Take time now to give God praise for His sovereign care over your life.

6. The author makes the point that even though God granted permission to Satan to test Job, God remained in complete control of the process. When you think of the severe testings in your own life, does that thought bring you any comfort? Why or why not?

# Chapter 3: Not a Chance

1. J. I. Packer says that believers can be comforted in the knowledge that each event of their lives "comes as a new summons to *trust, obey* and *rejoice,* knowing that all is for one's spiritual and eternal good." Think back to some difficult or devastating event in your life. How might things have turned out differently if you had viewed it in the way he described?

2. *"If God is in charge of everything in my life, and evil happens in my life, then isn't God responsible for evil? Doesn't that make Him the author of evil?"* Based on what you have learned in this chapter, how would you answer someone who asked you those two questions?

3. Since God is sovereign, in what sense are you still responsible for your own choices and decisions?

4. *"He owns it all, He rules over all, He has ordained all, He controls it all."* Name some circumstances of life where the assurance of those words could be very encouraging and comforting.

5. *Random* was recently a popular term with the younger generation. Somehow, it seemed to reflect a shrug-the-shoulders "whatever" outlook on life. Imagine waking up one morning with the conviction that everything in your life was random. How would that affect your attitude toward the events of your day? Now, conversely, how would your attitude change to realize that there truly are no random events in life, and that everything happens for a reason?

6. In Isaiah 44, the Lord speaks of a king named Cyrus who would be instrumental in allowing God's people to return to Jerusalem and Judah from Babylonian captivity. However, as the author points out, this prediction took place many years before that king was born—and even before Babylon conquered Judah. If you had this truth—God's foreknowledge of world events—firmly fixed in your mind, how might it change the way you read newspaper headlines or respond to the evening news?

## Chapter 4: Take This Job and Shovel It

1. Psalm 37:23 says, "The steps of a man are established by the LORD." The author concludes, "God is in control of your journey and of your destination … *right now.*" Apply that truth to the events of this very day. Does the author's statement seem like a stretch to you? Presuming his conclusion is true, what additional perspective does that give you about today's varied happenings?

2. "In God's plan, there are no wasted assignments. In God's plan, every assignment is preparation." What do you like and/or dislike about your present assignment? In what sense might it be preparing you for something else God has for you down the road?

3. How do you respond to the statement "Sometimes God will give you a dead-end assignment"? If you have found yourself in such a place, have you found it difficult to trust God's reasons for leaving you there for a time? How would you counsel a friend (or son or daughter) who finds himself or herself in such a place right now?

4. The author writes, "Every dead-end place and dead-end assignment has a beginning, a middle, and an end. God has set borders around your dead-end place. He has lessons for you to learn in the dead-end place that can be learned nowhere else." What types of lessons have you learned in your dead-end places?

5. The author states, "If the Lord is with you, all bets are off. Everything changes. Anything becomes possible." When we find ourselves dead-ended in life, where do we put our focus? Do we put it into trying every route possible to escape, or do we focus on the Lord, looking for His hand in our circumstances? Why is the latter course so difficult at times?

6. The chapter speaks of God's giving Joseph "an assignment within an assignment." What were those assignments? Speculate about God's possible assignment within an assignment for where He has you right now.

# Chapter 5: Sacked by God for a Ten-Yard Loss

1. When our well-laid plans have been turned upside down, we may find ourselves lost or disoriented. How does the Word of God stabilize us and redirect us after we absorb a grievous setback?

2. It was devastating for Joseph to gain success and power—against all odds—only to suddenly lose everything *again*. At what time in your life have you felt the same way? Did you turn to God during that time, or did you try to rely on your own strength to push through? If the former, how did God help you?

3. The author notes that God had so much more in mind for Joseph than he could have ever imagined. Did He ever! Take a moment to read the prayer in Ephesians 3:14–20—preferably in more than one translation. Take time to ponder the phrase "immeasurably more than all we ask or imagine." In what area of your life and your circumstances might you be limiting God right now?

4. Reflect on the statements "God is free to interrupt our plans at any time in order to achieve His superior plan in our lives. God has no problem in taking success away when it serves His purposes." Does this mean we shouldn't plan at all? How do we balance prudent planning with the understanding that God's plans take precedence?

5. First Timothy 4:16 (NIV) says, "Watch your life and doctrine closely." Commenting on this, the author says, "How we live our lives and what we believe about God and His Word must be watched very closely." Why does he say that? Why is it necessary to check our actions against our knowledge of the Bible?

6. *God is sovereign, but we are responsible.* Restate that unchanging fact of life in your own words.

# Chapter 6: When Hope Gets Intercepted

1. The author states, "Nothing kills the heart of a man more than the absence of hope." How can we keep hope alive in our hearts when the circumstances of life seem stacked against us?

2. Country singer Garth Brooks recorded a song titled "Some of God's Greatest Gifts Are Unanswered Prayers." Looking back, which prayers are you grateful that God in His wisdom never answered?

3. Broken hopes are tools in God's workshop to refine us and bring us the fruitful, overflowing life He desires for us. Let's imagine someone close to you experiences a deep disappointment, and comes to you for counsel. How might you encourage him or her in light of what you have learned in this chapter?

4. Through using Scripture, how would you encourage someone close to you who might be struggling with disappointment and dashed hopes?

5. Joseph, unjustly imprisoned, placed his hopes in the cupbearer who had been released from prison and restored to Pharaoh's service. What came of that opportunity? How do we balance the hopes we invest in people with an ongoing hope in the Lord?

6. The author notes, "The cupbearer would indeed turn out to be Joseph's get-out-of-jail-free card. But Joseph wouldn't hear a thing about it for two long years." Joseph, it seems, had the "what" right and the "who" right, but he didn't have the "when" right. Why would God delay an answer to our prayers when He fully intends for us to have that answer?

# Chapter 7: Demoted and Benched

1. The author writes, "We're sometimes compelled to wait in uncomfortable, uneasy circumstances, where the outcome is far from certain." What sorts of disciplines or daily activities might help us hold onto our faith when we're in a situation like this?

2. Open your Bible to the psalms, and read 25:3; 27:14; 37:7, 34; 62:5; 147:11. Then look over at Isaiah 40:31. What does the Word of God promise for those who wait patiently on the Lord?

3. Andrew Murray once wrote, "Let me say I am here by God's appointment, in His keeping, under His training, and for His time." Which of those aspects of waiting bring you the most comfort and encouragement right now?

4. The author writes about those times when God asks us to wait for the answer to our urgent prayers. He says, "Why not just give the frustration over to Him and trust that He knows best. Go ahead. Put this book down, bow your head, and give it over to Him. Tell Him what's on your heart. Get the anger out of your system, and then tell Him that you're willing to wait—even though you can't understand the reasons for it." What answer to a prayer are you waiting on right now? Have you been patient in waiting for the answer?

5. The author quotes the following verses as evidence that the Lord will sustain us and keep us as we wait for Him to answer our prayer or deliver us from a troubling situation. Take time to look them up again in your Bible (Ps. 28:9; 48:14; Isa. 46:3–4). What is the central promise in each of these passages?

6. What are the dangers of refusing to wait for the Lord's timing and bulling ahead on our own schedule and in our own wisdom?

# Chapter 8: Powerful Punks

1. The author writes, "It's the most comforting thing in all the world to know that there is a God who is in charge of my life." How do we as believers cooperate with Him and His plan in order to enjoy the maximum benefit?

2. How would you use Proverbs 21:1 and the story of Nebuchadnezzar in Daniel 4 to answer someone who doesn't believe that God would ever override man's free will?

3. The author writes, "Our sovereign God is the One who raises men and women to prominence and power, and just as quickly removes them." How might this statement give you perspective about the political tennis matches that go on in our country?

4. Instead of worrying about terrorism, nuclear attack, and evil empires in our world, the author suggests reading Isaiah 40 before bedtime. What specifics in that chapter might help you set aside such worries and simply rest in God?

5. "Pharaoh was about to cooperate with the plan of God," the author writes, "simply because he needed to get some sleep." And that was the night when God sent him dreams that would impact his own destiny. What other examples can you think of where powerful people are dependent upon God whether they acknowledge Him or not?

6. Theodore Roosevelt had a nightly routine of looking at the stars to remind himself of his own smallness and the greatness of God. What daily routine could you come up with to remind yourself that your destiny, trials, and opportunities lie in the hand of a sovereign God who loves you?

# Chapter 9: He Programs the Weather Channel

1. "The God of the Bible is knowable, but He is also incomprehensible." Is that a contradictory statement? Why or why not?

2. The author writes, "We must be very careful of charging God with evil when He uses evil for His good purposes that we are not able to comprehend." Obviously, when we find ourselves assaulted by some evil or tragedy, we want to understand what God is doing. How do we balance our desire for understanding with faith in a God who often works in ways beyond our understanding?

3. Look up Exodus 4:11 in your Bible. What further insight do you gain about this passage by comparing it with the story of the man born blind in John 9:1–5?

4. The author says this of his friend with a terminal disease: "He knows that death is coming and that God has already planned the precise moment of his passing (Heb. 9:27). He is at peace with his future because he knows that God has planned his future." Look up Job 21:21; Acts 13:36; and Hebrews 9:27. What do these verses indicate about the timing of our death? Does it comfort you to know that God knows the precise instant of your passing from earth? Why or why not?

5. Why might using the words "God is in control" cause distress rather than comfort when spoken to a grieving friend? What words (if you must use words at all) might be more helpful?

6. Margaret Clarkson says, "The circumstances surrounding our lives are no accident; they may be the work of evil, but that evil is held firmly within the mighty hand of our sovereign God.... All evil is subject to Him, and evil cannot touch His children unless He permits it." Evil that touches our lives, however, is *still* evil. Is it really a comfort to realize that evil can't touch us unless God permits it? Why or why not?

# Chapter 10: Climbing the Egyptian Ladder

1. The author writes, "If you serve a God who is in control of everything, including promotion, then you don't need to falsify your résumé to make yourself look better." Think back over the "promotions" in your life. In what ways can you see God's hand behind those advancements?

2. In a matter of a couple of hours, the whole course of Joseph's life changed dramatically and permanently. A door of opportunity suddenly swung wide open, and though he was undoubtedly surprised, he was ready to step through that door. What does that say to you about walking with the Lord moment by moment and being ready on the instant to change direction or seize a God-sent opportunity?

3. Joseph experienced a *"prompt promotion,* as a result of his being *properly positioned* by God after a long season of *patient preparation,* which included a significant test where Joseph was *purposely purified."* Where would you place yourself in the progression described above?

4. You may find yourself right now in a lengthy period of "preparation." Nothing seems to be happening, and you can't see any changes or improvements on the horizon. What specific points of encouragement do you draw from Hebrews 12:1–12?

5. The author writes, "Hardships and afflictions come straight from the hand of an infinitely loving heavenly Father—and are designed to deepen us and strengthen us and give us the endurance we need for the work that lies ahead of us." Read Romans 5:1–6. How does the apostle describe the strengthening of a believer's faith through difficult trials?

6. Imagine you are a parent trying to explain to an adolescent son or daughter how God can use disappointments and trials to prepare him or her for wonderful opportunities in the future. What words might you use to simply convey this concept?

# Chapter 11: From Womb to Tomb

1. The author gives the example of Captain Robert FitzRoy, and how his life was destroyed by taking responsibility for the evil eventually brought into this world by Charles Darwin. How might FitzRoy have been helped by meditating on Bible verses such as Genesis 50:20 and Romans 8:28?

2. Compare what Joseph said to his brothers in Genesis 50:20 about "this present result" with the Lord's words in Matthew 5:10–12. Can we always expect God to turn an unjust situation around in our lifetime? What does Jesus say about God's recompense beyond our years on earth?

3. The author states, "There is nothing more astonishing about the providence of God than this: He is able to take the evil that comes against you and wounds you and those near to you, and He promises to work it out for good." How have you seen that play out in your own life? How would you use that truth to counsel and comfort someone who has been wounded by an unjust attack?

4. Joseph named his two sons Manasseh and Ephraim. The names mean "for-getting" and "twice fruitful." How do these two names describe Joseph's God-ordained promotion and sudden prosperity?

5. In Stephen's final speech before he was murdered by a mob, he cited the example of Joseph and how God rescued him from evil (Acts 7:9–10). Yet Stephen was *not* rescued. How do you reconcile the truths that God can and sometimes does deliver His children from earthly evil, but not always?

6. Quoting Romans 11:33, that God's ways are "past finding out," Thomas Watson observed that the ways of the Lord "are rather to be admired than fathomed." Have you come to the place in life where you can praise God for difficult circumstances that you can't begin to understand? What step of faith could you take right now to demonstrate to God that you will trust His heart, even when you can't trace His ways?

# Notes

## Chapter 1

1. Sinclair B. Ferguson, David F. Wright, J. I. Packer, eds., *New Dictionary of Theology* (Downers Grove, IL: InterVarsity Press, 1988), 654.

2. Benjamin B. Warfield, *The Christian Workers Magazine*, December 1916, 265–67, homepage.mac.com/shanerosenthal/reformationlink/bbwpredest. htm. (Accessed March 17, 2008.)

3. John J. Murray, *Behind a Frowning Providence* (Carlisle, PA: The Banner of Truth Trust, 1990), 10.

4. Wayne Grudem, *Bible Doctrine: Essential Teachings of the Christian Faith* (Grand Rapids, MI: Zondervan, 1999), 143.

5. David Halberstam, *The Education of a Coach* (New York: Hyperion, 2005), 2.

6. Ibid., 3–4.

## Chapter 2

1. Benjamin B. Warfield, *The Christian Workers Magazine*, December 1916, 265–67, homepage.mac.com/shanerosenthal/reformationlink/bbwpredest. htm. (Accessed March 17, 2008.)

2. Martin Gilbert, *Churchill: A Life* (New York: Henry Holt and Company, 1991), 956.

3. www.geocities.com/dwwsmw56/Astoria.html. (Accessed March 17, 2008.)

4. I. D. E. Thomas, *A Puritan Golden Treasury* (Carlisle, PA: The Banner of Truth Trust, 1977), 230.

5. Walter Bruce Davis, *William Carey: Father of Modern Missions* (Chicago: Moody Press, 1963), 58.

6. J. D. Douglas and Philip W. Comfort, eds., *Who's Who in Christian History* (Wheaton, IL: Tyndale, 1992), 132.

7. C. Murray, as quoted in F. B. Meyer, *Patriarchs of the Faith* (Chattanooga, TN: AMG Publishers, 1995), 333.

## Chapter 3

1. www.hoover.org/publications/policyreview/2930951.html. (Accessed March 17, 2008.)

2. James Bradley, *Flyboys* (Boston: Little, Brown and Company, 2003), 194–97.

3. Ibid., 197.

4. J. I. Packer, *Concise Theology* (Wheaton, IL: Tyndale, 1993), 33.

5. D. Martyn Lloyd-Jones, *Great Doctrines of the Bible,* vol. 1, *God the Father, God the Son* (Wheaton, IL: Crossway, 1996), 150.

6. John M. Frame, *The Doctrine of God* (Phillipsburg, PA: P&R Publishing, 2002), 59.

## Chapter 4

1. F. B. Meyer, *Great Men of the Bible,* vol. 1 (Grand Rapids, MI: Zondervan, 1981), 115.

2. Stephen E. Ambrose, *Eisenhower: Soldier and President* (New York: Simon and Schuster, 1990), 11–12.

3. Ibid., 59.

4. Ibid., 53.

5. Ibid., 44.

6. Ibid., 48.

7. C. H. Spurgeon, *The Treasury of David,* vol. 2 (Pasadena, TX: Pilgrim, 1983), 189.

8. Ambrose, *Eisenhower,* 34.

# Chapter 5

1. Glen N. Landrum, *Profiles of Genius* (Buffalo, NY: Prometheus, 1993), 91.

2. Gene Edward Veith, *A Place to Stand: The Word of God in the Life of Martin Luther* (Nashville: Cumberland, 2005), 101.

3. Ravi Zacharias, *Walking from East to West* (Grand Rapids, MI: Zondervan, 2006), 139–41.

4. William Manchester, *The Last Lion* (New York: Dell Publishing, 1983), 781.

5. Veith, *Place to Stand,* 70.

6. Ibid., 71.

7. Ibid., 77.

# Chapter 6

1. Glen N. Landrum, *Profiles of Genius* (Buffalo, NY: Prometheus, 1993), 161.

2. Ibid.

3. John Flavel, *The Mystery of Providence* (Carlisle, PA: The Banner of Truth Trust, 1678), 32.

4. Harold Myra and Marshall Shelley, *The Leadership Secrets of Billy Graham* (Grand Rapids, MI: Zondervan, 2005), 59.

5. Paul Johnson, *A History of the American People* (New York: Harper Perennial, 1997), 438.

6. Steve Saint, *End of the Spear* (Carol Stream, IL: SaltRiver, 2005), 59–60.

# Chapter 7

1. Robert J. Morgan, *The Red Sea Rules* (Nashville: Thomas Nelson, 2001), 86–87.

2. Ibid., 13.

3. Rocky McElveen, *Wild Men, Wild Alaska* (Nashville: Thomas Nelson, 2006), 5.

4. Ibid., 158.

5. Ibid.

6. Ibid., 159.

7. Ibid., 162–63.

8. Morgan, *Red Sea Rules,* 13.

# Chapter 8

1. Christopher Hitchens, *God Is Not Great: Why Religion Poisons Everything* (New York: Twelve, 2007), 15–16.

2. Jerry Bridges, *Is God Really in Control?* (Colorado Springs: NavPress, 2006), 29.

3. Greg Boyd, as quoted in Jerry Bridges, *Is God Really in Control?* (Colorado Springs: NavPress, 2006), 28.

4. Robert A. Caro, *The Power Broker* (New York: Random House, 1974), back cover.

5. Sir John Glubb, as quoted in Guy R. Odom, *Mothers, Leadership and Success* (Houston: Polybius, 1990), 186.

6. http://dariusthemede.tripod.com/glubb. (Accessed March 17, 2008.)

7. George Grant, *Carry a Big Stick: The Uncommon Heroism of Theodore Roosevelt* (Nashville: Cumberland, 1996), 176.

8. Ibid., 126.

# Chapter 9

1. www.elizabethi.org/us/armada. (Accessed March 17, 2008.)

2. www.desiringgod.org/ResourceLibrary/Sermons/ByDate/2005/223_The_Supremacy_of_Christ_in_an_Age_of_Terror. (Accessed March 17, 2008.)

3. Jerry Bridges, *Is God Really in Control?* (Colorado Springs: NavPress, 2006), 58–59.

4. Bruce A. Ware, *God's Greater Glory* (Wheaton, IL: Crossway, 2004), 72.

5. Ibid., 70–71.

6. Ibid., 100, 102. Obviously we cannot, in the pages of this book, explore every question and nuance of God's sovereignty and how that works with evil. That would take more than a book, and more than a library. I would strongly suggest for those of you who want to study this concept in more detail that you get a copy of *God's Greater Glory* by Dr. Bruce Ware, a carefully reasoned, Bible-drenched work on the providence of God. In fact, I would suggest that you get two copies—the additional copy would be a gift for your pastor. It would be a gift that would be greatly appreciated.

7. www.alertnet.org/thenews/newsdesk/L08160754.htm. (Accessed March 17, 2008.)

8. Ware, *God's Greater Glory,* 106–7.

9. As quoted in Bridges, *Is God Really in Control?* 61.

10. David McCullough, *1776* (New York: Simon and Schuster, 2005), 191.

11. Ibid.

12. Warren W. Wiersbe, *The Bible Exposition Commentary: Pentateuch* (Colorado Springs: Victor, 2001), 192.

13. As quoted in Bridges, *Is God Really in Control?* 31.

## Chapter 10

1. www.forbes.com/leadership/2007/92/07leadership-resume-jobs-lead-careers-cx_ll_0207resume.html?partner=rss. (Accessed July 14, 2007.)

2. Thomas Watson, *All Things for Good* (Carlisle, PA: The Banner of Truth Trust, 1663, 1986), 60.

3. John Piper, *The Roots of Endurance* (Wheaton, IL: Crossway, 2002), 124.

4. Ibid., 125.

5. D. Martyn Lloyd-Jones, *Spiritual Depression* (Grand Rapids, MI: W. B. Eerdmans, 1965), 158.

6. F. B. Meyer, *The Life of Joseph* (Seattle: YWAM, 1995), 43.

7. Kevin Belmonte, *Hero for Humanity: A Biography of William Wilberforce* (Colorado Springs: NavPress, 2002), 102.

8. Ibid., inside cover flap.

9. Ibid., 11.

10. Piper, *Roots of Endurance,* 117.

11. Ibid.

12. Meyer, *Patriarchs of the Faith,* 381.

## Chapter 11

1. Paul Johnson, *Modern Times: The Word from the Twenties to the Nineties*, rev. ed. (New York: Harper Perennial, 1991), 341.

2. Os Guinness, *Unspeakable: Facing Up to Evil in an Age of Genocide and Terror* (New York: HarperSanFrancisco, 2005), introductory page.

3. Ibid., xi.

4. Thomas Watson, *All Things for Good* (Carlisle, PA: The Banner of Truth Trust, 1663, 1986), 60–61.

5. Warren W. Wiersbe, *The Bible Exposition Commentary: Pentateuch* (Colorado Springs: Victor, 2001), 150.

6. R. C. Sproul, *The Invisible Hand* (Dallas: Word, 1996), 95.

7. John Rylands, as quoted in J. I. Packer, *God's Plans for You* (Wheaton, IL: Crossway, 2001), 9.